Advice to Kublai Khan

Letters by the Tibetan Monk Chogyal Phagpa

To Kublai Khan and his Court

Translations by

Christopher Wilkinson

2015

Chogyal Phagpa

No part of this book may be reproduced in any form or by any electronic or mechanical means including information storage and retrieval systems, without permission in writing from the author. The only exception is by a reviewer, who may quote excerpts in a review.

Cover Image: Copy of Portrait of Kublai Khan by Anige done in 1294 cropped out of a page from an album depicting several Yuan emperors (Yuandai di banshenxiang), original now located in the National Palace Museum in Taipei (inv. nr. zhonghua 000324). Original size is 47 cm wide and 59.4 cm high. Paint and ink on silk. For the full page, see Image:YuanEmperorAlbumKhubilaiFull.jpg. Source: Artdaily.org. *This work is in the public domain in the United States, and those countries with a copyright term of life of the author plus 100 years or less. This file has been identified as being free of known restrictions under copyright law, including all related and neighboring rights.*

Page URL: http://commons.wikimedia.org/wiki/File%3AYuanEmperorAlbumKhubilaiPortrait.jpg.

File URL: http://upload.wikimedia.org/wikipedia/commons/1/1b/YuanEmperorAlbumKhubilaiPortrait.jpg.

Published by Christopher Wilkinson

Cambridge, MA, USA

Advice to Kublai Khan

Copyright © 2015 Christopher Wilkinson

All rights reserved.

ISBN: 1511513438
ISBN-13: 978-1511513432

Chogyal Phagpa

ALSO TRANSLATED BY CHRISTOPHER WILKINSON

The Great Tantra of Vajrasattva: Equal to the End of the Sky

Secret Wisdom: Three Root Tantras of the Great Perfection

Beyond Wisdom: The Upadesha of Vairochana on the Practice of the Great Perfection

The Sakya Kongma Series:

Sakya Pandita's Poetic Wisdom

Jetsun Dragpa Gyaltsan: The Hermit King

Admission at Dharma's Gates by Sonam Tsemo

An Overview of Tantra and Related Works

Chogyal Phagpa: The Emperor's Guru

CONTENTS

	Acknowledgments	ix
1	Introduction	11
2	Kublai's Exemplary Sponsorship of the Precious Scriptures	13
3	A Rosary of Gemstones: A Discourse for Prince Jibig Timur	19
4	The Stages of Practice in Brilliant Clarity: Written for Duchess Pundari	49
5	A Brilliant Letter to Prince Nomo Khan	59
6	A Rosary of Beneficence: A Discourse for Prince Manggala	73
7	Light Rays from the Moon: Confidential Advice for Prince Demur Bhoga	105
8	A Fountain of Ambrosia: Confidential Advice for Prince Degus Bhoga	111
9	Advise for King Hoko	121
10	Talking About Shame for Bad Ways of Practice	135
11	The Heart Essence of the Path to Enlightenment	139
12	The Way to Restore Memory	147
13	A Letter to Atsara	149
14	An Excellent Work of Advice for the King	151
15	An Ornament to Illuminate the Orations: A Presentation on the Excellent Work of Advice for the King	163
16	An Outline of My Advice to the King	239
	About the Translator	245

DEDICATION

For my son, Wes.

ACKNOWLEDGMENTS

The present work brings together inspirations and encouragement I have received over the past forty years from many remarkable people, too many to name. I would like to express very special thanks, first to my mother, for everything. My guru, Dezhung Rinpoche, is my direct inspiration. He read the entire contents of the Sakya Kabum out loud to me. He empowered, taught, and discussed the contents with me personally over many years. Many lamas of the Tibetan tradition were critical to my training and study. I want to make special thanks to H.H. Sakya Trizin, Jigdral Sakya, Ngawang Kunga Trinlay Sakyapa, Luding Khen, Chopgye Trichen, Dhongthog Rinpoche, H.H. Karmapa Rangjung Rigpay Dorje, Kalu Rinpoche, Chogyam Trungpa, Dilgo Khyentse, Khenpo Palden Sherab, and Geshe Ngawang Nornang for their kindness in teaching and encouraging me. All of these people are precious, and all have made precious contributions to my ability to offer these translations. Many great scholars and practitioners of the West have helped me to gain the skills and experience to bring this works into fluent and accurate English. I wish to make special thanks to David Ruegg, Turrell Wylie, Gene Smith, Karen Lang, Anne MacDonald, Richard Solomon, Jack Hawley, David Jackson, Cyrus Stearns, Leonard van der Kuijp, Eva Neumeier-Dargyay, Leslie Kawamura, Robert Thurman, Paul Hackett, Paul Nietupski, Lou Lancaster, David Snellgrove, Jean-Luc Achard, Steve Landsberg, Moke Mokotoff, Tsultrim Alione, Carolyn Klein, Donald Rubin, Rob Mayer, Jonathan Silk, David White, Mark Tatz, Steve Goodman, Kennard Lipman, Karen Louise White, Adeline Lim, Jill Sudbury, and Rory Lindsay. I wish to especially thank Merrill Peterson, Sarah Moosvi, and Otavio Lilla for proofing the manuscript. These translations originally appeared as a serialized release on Facebook. Many friends, too many to count, contributed to their realization by reading, sharing, contemplating, and supporting this work. I thank every one of them. The many people who have contributed to my understanding and ability to do this work cannot be counted. I wish to thank everyone that has taken a kind interest in these translations, however slight, for your part in making this work a reality.

INTRODUCTION

When the Mongol Empire was at its height it controlled the world from China and Korea to Russia on into Eastern Europe, South-east Asia, and Persia. It was during this period that a ten year old Tibetan child, Phagpa (1235-1280), was taken to the court of the Khans. Educated there by his uncle, Sakya Pandita, he grew up speaking both Mongolian and Tibetan. While in his twenties, he created the first written alphabet for the Mongolian language. He became a religious advisor to Kublai Khan, and officiated at his installation as Emperor. As Kublai Khan had granted him regencies over the thirteen myriarchies of Tibet, he was titled *Chogyal*, or "Dharma King." He was on familiar enough terms with the leaders of the Mongol empire, including Kublai Khan, that he wrote letters to them.

These letters are documents of state that offer us a window into the Yuan Dynasty. Phagpa, as a monk, exhorts the Khans to understand the ways of Buddhism, and also speaks out on such practices as massacre and the chopping off of hands. He speaks out for the right of public assembly. He presents economic theories regarding the taxation of the populace, while decrying the seizure of assets. While doing these things, he also speaks to the personal concerns and situation of his readers. We read of the despair of Duchess Pundari, for example, whose good husband had died unexpectedly and whose wealth was being stolen.

These letters, being written in a world where many religions were known and to readers who were not necessarily sympathetic to Buddhism, also offer us brilliant presentations of Buddhist ideas as they were taught to non-Buddhists. The larger part of Tibetan Buddhist literature was written by and for scholars in the tradition. Here we have preserved Buddhist teachings intended for an audience not already familiar with the tradition.

The *Advice for King Hoko*, for example, gives a detailed explanation of the Buddhist view on the structure and development of the universe.

While these letters were addressed to only one individual, a member of the Mongol Court, they were written with an understanding that they would be read by many. Because of the brilliant presentation each represents, they have become texts used for teaching by Tibetan Lamas through the centuries, and even today we will hear of Lamas giving seminars focused on these letters. I hope that these translations will also serve to give communities who study the Dharma a reliable text to work from.

These letters are noteworthy due to their content, but it is also worth noting that they are composed in Tibetan. Phagpa was fluent in Mongolian and had created its alphabet. The Khans were not fluent in Tibetan. Phagpa could not have expected the Mongol rulers to read and understand his letters unless he had also included a Mongolian translation. These letters are not written as notes to be translated, however, but use a highly literary style of Tibetan. I hope that scholars working in Mongolian studies will be inspired to investigate whether any Mongolian translations of these letters exist.

I have included Phagpa's *Heart Essence of the Path to Enlightenment*, as it shows us the kind of Buddhist practice he was recommending to his listeners, and a few of his short poems. The *Excellent Work of Advice for the King* gives us personal advice that reached the Emperor's ears. Kublai Khan repeatedly requested Phagpa to write a commentary on it, and this commentary is translated here along with the letter of advice. This work stands alone as a remarkable contribution to the literary heritage of the Buddhist tradition. I hope that by making it available in English, a broader and deeper understanding of the impact of Buddhism in civilizing the Mongol Empire will be gained by all.

Thank you for your interest in these unique historical and religious documents.

Chris Wilkinson
April, 2015

Advice to Kublai Khan

KUBLAI'S EXEMPLARY SPONSORSHIP OF THE PRECIOUS SCRIPTURES

Go pe las rgyas 'bring bsdus gsum bshengs pa'i mtshon byed

I bow to all the Buddhas and Bodhisattvas.

The true spirit of all holy gurus
Is the unified alliance of all the Buddhas,
For none are higher.
They grant us all the fruits of their glory,
For none are higher.
I bow to this community of gurus,
For none are higher.

The Buddha is the finest lantern.
He illuminates the world,
Along with its gods,
And a hundred divinities offer their crown jewels
At his feet.
He overwhelms the asuras,
Along with their troops.
He is the god of the gods,
The supreme deity.
He is victorious.

The Dharma is virtuous
In the beginning, during the interim, and in the end.
The vision of the Dharma
Shines through atoms and through the darkness,
And through anything that is not the Dharma.
It propagates the glory of peace.
The good Dharma grants certitude.
I bow to this path.

The oceanic Sangha
Is well-born from out of the practice of virtue,
Which is its source.
It represents a unified motion on the path of goodness and virtue.
Virtue prospers in the massive clouds of its ocean.
So I bow to them,
And offer them gifts.

All the things that appear to be
A multiplicity of created and terminated entities
Have been well demonstrated to occur within a dimension
In which there is no creation or termination.
The mother of the Victorious Ones was never born.
She is totally free from the limitations
Of this world and of its peace,
Of creation and of everything else.
I bow to her.

Now when the time had come
In which the lives of the populace
Whose fortune was good,
The most fortunate of all,
Were a hundred years,
The King of the Śākyas appeared
As a King of the Dharma.
He stated his precious orations clearly
To those who were alive.

Then, in the seventh five hundred year period
During which his teachings were taught,
The Hor tribe appeared in the Northern part of Jambu Island,
Which is symbolized by the jambu fruit.
They overwhelmed the other tribes.
The most famous Genghis Khan

Advice to Kublai Khan

Used his magnificent repute,
As well as his own forces,
To bring all the nations under his control.

Five royal successions after him,
It was everywhere proclaimed to those who were alive
That Kublai is the highest king.
He has used royal expedients to make his government flourish,
Even greater than the greatness of yore,
And it has indeed expanded,
As befits the Dharma.
He has endowed those who are alive
With both glory and possessions.

This lord of the earth has a brilliant respect for the teachings,
And a special love of the heart for the regions of Tibet.
So he has employed himself at vast projects
To organize the protection of the land of snow.

To everyone's benefit,
He granted one called: "Tontsul"[1] full empowerment
As the leader of everyone in the province of Dokham[2]
Called: "Zalmo Gang,"[3]
And its districts to the East, West, South, and North.

He, in turn, appointed one called: "Ganimdu," of the Uighur tribe,
Who was born in the castle of Gara Gojo,
And has a son named Dugal Gaya,
Whose home companion is the woman Durmis Derim,
Their son being Yugrun Gaya,
Whose younger brother is Ze'un Gaya,
The youngest brother being Esena,
To protect his friends, the country, and the province,
And gave him oral instructions, letters of authority, and a seal,
Making this act of investiture successful.

His guru was one who illuminated the three worlds.
He was a guide for the three realms,

---

[1] sTon tshul. This person is mentioned by Sakya Pandita in his Letter to the Abbot of Sho Monastery and also in another poem by Phagpa, In Praise of Friendship.
[2] mDo khams
[3] Zal mo sgang

A teacher of the three paths,
And was well-known by the name: "Sakya Pandita."
It was through his kindness
That the Khan was brilliantly brought in to the teachings,
And was instructed.

So in an effort to attain Buddhahood,
Which is what we must succeed in doing,
And so that the king his sons, and their wives
Might have long lives,
And so that their government might be stable,
And so that they might repay their parents' kindness,
And so that their kingdom might be blessed by the Dharma,
He summoned the unions of those skilled in the crafts
To a place called Markham Tsomdo,[4]
In the third month of autumn during the male wood dog year,[5]
To publish the Perfection of Wisdom: Vast, middling, and brief,
Which is the mother of the Victorious Ones of the three times.

He commissioned it to be done properly,
Using fine gold that had been melted
Into a parchment that resembles *vaiḍūrya*.
Moreover, he magnified the service performed
By having the work reviewed for corrections,
Making wooden covers and binding straps,
And wrapping them in silken covers.
Then they performed an entirely consummate consecration,
According to the methods described in the stainless transmission.
As compensation he offered them stores of virtuous commodities
Nothing being unmentionable.

He offered these things as a supreme field of merit,
Where the Dharma would be properly studied
And integrated into our hearts,
So that its virtues would flourish,
And its transmission be prolonged thereafter.

He also used his higher thinking
To organize events for reading
And to make extensive offerings of recitations

---

[4] sMar Khams tsom mdo
[5] 1274/75 A.D

Advice to Kublai Khan

In which these oceanic virtues
And all the virtues there are
Throughout the three times and ten directions
Would be brought in a unity.

So may I, and all these sentient beings,
Equal to the sky,
Attain the holiness of perfect enlightenment,
And, under the present circumstances,
May these lords of the earth, father and sons,
Have long lives.
May their kingdom be endowed with the Dharma,
And may goodness and virtue prevail.

My I personally have a long life without illness,
And may the things that obstruct me be pacified.
May all my wishes come true,
As befits the Dharma,
And when this undefeated king
Actually is enlightened
May he show his transmission of enlightenment to be holy.

So it is that this poem,
The function of which is to present something significant,
Was well-written in the land of Tsomdo
On the fifteenth day of the month of the cock[6]
In the year of the female wood pig (1275/76 A.D.).
May there be happiness and goodness for us all.

---

[6] Bya sbo

Chogyal Phagpa

A ROSARY OF GEMSTONES:
A DISCOURSE FOR PRINCE JIBIG TIMUR

rGyal bu ji big de mur la gtam du bya ba nor bu'i phreng ba

I bow to all the Buddhas and Bodhisattvas.

The king of the mountains was brilliantly born
From out of an ocean of merit.
His body is magnified by a store of wisdom.
It is adorned with innumerable wonders.
I bow to it.

You were born as an island
In an ocean of virtue.
You hold the splendors of tribe, physique, and endowments,
And glory in the protection of your own life.
O Prince of Jewels,
May you be victorious.

This letter comes out of Phagpa's intelligence,
For he is one who teaches the rule of the way as a ground of purity.
He maintains a reservoir of great learning,
And holds a collection of wondrous precious jewels.
It is a rosary of gemstones
That casts clear light in every direction,
An ornament that will foster beauty
In ourselves and in others.
With thoughts of virtue,
I offer it from afar.

You have a perfect store of glory and endowments,
So what will you do with your life?
I offer you a life of Dharma that will make you shine,
Just as the autumn moon does for jasmine.

One who has a perfect store of glory,
But does not maintain the glory of the Dharma,
Will only propagate sorrow.
This is like eating fine food that is mixed with poison.

One who has the glory of the Dharma,
But becomes isolated on account of the glories of the world,
Will be of no help for anyone else.
This is like a precious jewel encased in a shell.

One who has a perfect store of both of these
Will succeed in their grand objectives,
Both for themselves and others.
This is how precious jewels, when handled skillfully,
Naturally make things beautiful.

For someone who has these two kinds of glory
This is the fruition of everything,
So this is for you.
Focus your thinking on what I say here.

The light of the sun,
The oceans expanse,
And the stability of the mountains
Will fail at the end of time.
The possessions of those who live are not worth mentioning.

When you know that this is so
Your heart will not be haughty
On account of your glories.
You will use your glory to make glory grow.
To do this, constantly seek the support of those with propriety.

Constantly ponder how sorrow appears within our hearts,
The maintenance of a Dharma that will bring about happiness,
How everything emerges from out of a cause,
And how to use this cause toward virtuous conditions

Advice to Kublai Khan

That will keep your own tormented heart, and those of others,
From being entirely obsessed in emotions.

Use the real and transmitted strength of your community,
And the prayers of their accord,
To consider the kindness of your parents and their lineage
In giving birth to your person.

Practice virtue in the tradition of the way
So that their lineal descendants will be like a river,
And so that you will fulfill their wishes,
Just as they intended.

Forever esteem the virtuous ones
Whose glory you truly rely on,
And whose kindness you have received,
As if they were your crown jewel.

They are like precious jewels for you,
Granting you everything that you wish for,
With no exceptions,
And make it fitting that others who are alive
Should honor you.

Within your clan there are old people.
Among professors there are those who speak the truth.
Among scriptural traditions there are those that maintain what is fitting.
Among the austere there are those who are useful to others.
Among the wealthy there are those who are wise.
Among the polite there are those who maintain what is good.
Among the lowly there are those who are miserable.
Among the miserable there are those who are sick.
Among your wives there are those who follow you.
Among your sons there are vision keepers.
Among your relatives there are those who do not deceive you.
Among your friends there are those who send help.
Among your slaves there are those who heed your orders.
Among those you have helped
There are those who remember your kindness.
Among those you have harmed there are those who are forgiving.
Among them all, there are those you will chance to encounter.

Please have consideration for all of them.
Honor them and protect them.
These conditions will make other people become active
In karmas that maintain the way.

Those who are harmful to other beings,
Such as fishermen and butchers,
Do not even succeed in helping themselves,
So what can we say about their help for others?

It is certainly true
That details with respect to their usefulness to others
Are confidentially employed
To assess students, children of the victorious ones, and victorious ones,
Following a structure of ignoble, average, or superior,
But when we employ concerns regarding their true usefulness
As being small, medium, or large,
Are we not observing only the most outstanding
Of those that are small, average, or great?

It follows that it is proper for you to have love in your heart
For embodied beings, however many there may be.
So why should we even try to talk about how proper it is
To love the people that depend on you?

You are endowed with a physical structure and a life,
The same way that everyone alive is.
This being so,
To slaughter some while you work for the contentment of some others
Is not the way of the Dharma.

The minds of the multitude
Are engaged in enticing dramas that make them happy,
And are harmless.
They remove our regrets.
It is proper that you relish in them
When the time is right,

But the minds of people who are entrenched in perversity
Inflict harm on the multitude
Just for some temporary delight.
When you scrutinize them,
You will know that they are sources of misery,

Advice to Kublai Khan

And you will get rid of them.

I have made mistakes,
But I do not tolerate cruel words for others.
What else is there to do then,
But oppose this slaughter of sentient beings who are harmless?

The way where we use a love for others toward our personal objectives,
Of protecting others in order to honor ourselves,
And of speaking out pleasantries to make praise for ourselves
Is the Dharma of material things.
Let's set aside a love for the objective of being enlightened
And the accomplishment of anything beneficial.
Are these kinds of attentiveness toward the objectives of the world
Not inappropriate?

Consider these things.
Work toward something beneficial,
And toward a love for other beings.
I expect that you will succeed,
In the present and in the future,
In all your objectives, and in those of others,
With no exceptions.

To augment your life, glory, and the Dharma
You must prioritize the problem areas.
Once you have reversed them,
I urge you to work earnestly
Toward turning away from these measures.

You must use your voice with thorough consideration
For the holy ones you call: "Protectors of the Holy Dharma,"
For they use their wealth, their lives, and everything they have
To guard your entourage and the bodies of your retinue.

Under some circumstances you will not succeed
In some of your objectives,
Be they of the Dharma or of the world,
But don't turn your heart on them.
Observe the ways of businesspeople and farmers.

It is extremely difficult to succeed
At the grand objectives that we must accomplish

All of a sudden,
But if we work for success progressively,
We will succeed, though they be difficult,
As are the castles of the ants.

A single act of opposition to the success of a vast labor
Will be multiplied.
A single arrow that bears poison
Will take the life of a living being.

The sands of the beneficent oceans do not grow in their numbers,
Regardless of how many there may be,
And regardless of how extensive a king's government may be,
It is not so grand, is it?

We may have expedients,
But the harm we do will fall on our own armies.
Use the intelligence by which mad elephants
Are controlled with iron hooks
Before they are led around.

The world professes the use of ferocious applications
To subdue our enemies,
But they will be pacified by peace.
This is like using water on fire, instead of fire.

We may use cruelties to overcome a single dangerous entity,
But later on it will have multiplied.
Consider how things turn out
When we remove a stone that bothers us
From a mound of pebbles.
When we control these things skillfully
They increase in support of our own position.

The dwellings of those who reside among mountains of stone,
Who live there as construction workers,
Are not fortified, are they?
Just so, as you take control of other places,
Take care for everyone there who has become your vassal,
As befits the Dharma.
Use the Dharma to make the worldly happy.

Advice to Kublai Khan

To do this, be friendly and speak pleasantly.
Make use of those whom you have granted appropriate status,
And those who are in search of effulgent finery,
To extend your government and its subjects.

As you extend them,
The glory and endowments that come out of their work
Will all become glories for you,
And they will all be united at the gates where they convene.

How could this be?
It is the same as when farmers strive to do business there on their farms,
There may be a harvest,
But they won't retain it, will they?

A government and its subjects may themselves be equal,
But when they are doing wrong or doing good,
You must try to terminate or favor them respectively,
As you would a physical disease or a sustenance.

To bring an end to them,
It is proper to rebuke them,
Beat them, deprive them, and denigrate them,
So as to drive them out,
But to take their lives from them is not so.

When clothes are covered in filth,
The wise will wash them before wearing them.
Who would claim that it is heroic
To burn them so that they are no more?

When we have granted due status,
And then revoke it,
We will have become traitors.
Consider the way we give food
To little children who have gotten sick.

In this world there is no one
Who has no virtues and has no faults.
We must adopt them or reject them
By scrutinizing which is predominant
And the temporary situation.

As with a smoky lantern,
A poison that tastes delicious,
A chariot that we use to cross over the plains
Or a boat to cross over the water,
We must understand how things are
With the ways of our possessions.

There are those that are our enemies,
Those that are our companions,
Those that are insignificant,
And, fourthly, those that are truly enjoyable.

Those that we start out seeking and collecting,
That we propagate and protect during the interim,
And are intrinsically harmful
Due to fights and disputes that lead to damage in the end
Are enemy possessions.

Material things that are pure,
That we have properly acquired or gotten spontaneously,
That through virtuous considerations
We use as gifts and offerings,
Are possessions that develop into benefits,
And therefore are companions.

Things that we acquire that are neither beneficial nor harmful,
That we do not use for gifts or for pleasure,
That we are constantly storing up or running out of,
Are possessions that are insignificant.

Things that we ourselves and others use
To make us happy in temporary situations,
Regardless of how we first acquire them,
Are the things that are enjoyable.

Now the first and the third of these
Must be forever relinquished.
The second should be thoroughly enjoyed.
The forth must be used purely,
In whatever way is appropriate.

When there is no satisfaction,
Possessions function as propagators of sorrow.

Advice to Kublai Khan

Consider the source from which
The loss of physical stamina and ulcerous sickness emerge.

Beer makes us despise the world.
Our bodies deteriorate and our intellects decline.
It makes us part from significant experience of the Dharma.
Observe how beer is always like a poison.

Furthermore, attachment to lust
Depletes the virtue we have accumulated,
And when we do it constantly we get worn out.
So always try to remain satisfied.

The wise way to accomplish what we are doing
Is to investigate before we engage.
Those who analyze after they engage
Are called fools.

Whatever your actions may be,
Investigate whether they are evidenced in the holy scriptures,
Confer on them,
Then implement them.
You will succeed in all your objectives.
Not only that,
You will have no regrets.

To sum it up,
Do not be arrogant or timid,
Be appreciative and have gratitude for kindnesses,
Make offerings to those worthy of gifts,
Protect the lowly,
Maintain control of opposing factions,
Protect the nation's environment,
Enjoy your possessions with dignity,
Engage in your works prudently,

When we do things this way,
Our stores will be perfect in this world.
This is due to our concern for the happiness of our opponents.
And so it is that I beg you to embark on the road of happiness.

There certainly are a great many teachers
Who will lead us on a variety of pathways.

They will claim to have overcome
The errors that are associated with their causes,
And to be supreme in the total perfection of their virtues,
While they say: "I am inferior in my virtue,
And that is why I have faults."
But who would not say such things?

Scrutinize their character with your mind.
Are their behaviors and their teachings
To be found, the way they do them,
In the scriptures?

The words spoken in the scriptures are stainless.
They have been certified through two kinds of validation.
They are devoid of contradictions and disconnected content.
They function in unison toward helpfulness and happiness.
These scriptural traditions are holy.
We don't see the likes of them elsewhere.
Our teacher released them on his own initiative,
And he is the best of teachers.

The people that embark upon the trails that he spoke of are also holy.
They are, in fact. the holy ones who continue to scrutinize,
Even though they have committed themselves to the Dharma,
And through their brilliant faith in the perfect Buddha
They have embarked on the trails of his children and students.

And so it is that you too may understand
The virtues there are in the corpus of the Buddha's Dharmas,
And you may have faith in them.
Then, so that you may protect us from all our fears,
I urge you to hereafter receive,
For so long as you may live and prosper,
The teachers and the path as friends,
For they are the finest of refuges.

They have done away with faults
And are a magnificent foundation for every virtue,
So it is that they demonstrate
That they are superior as refuges.
This is why I urge you to enter through these ambrosial gates,
And forever employ yourself as befits the Dharma.

Advice to Kublai Khan

The foundation for this, in turn,
Is the rule of the way.
Use the eight avenues for remaining abstinent
To work toward virtue every day.

Habituate yourself to pure morals,
And take them as your chosen deity.
This is what the Victorious One talked about.

Take vows to relinquish the lasciviousness and debauchery
You will encounter throughout your future lives,
And use them to be pure in everything you do,
For they will emancipate you as an individual.

Even though you might not practice them in complete perfection,
I urge you to rely on them as is fitting,
No matter what.
Even though you might practice just a single one of them,
Your austerities will be beautified by it.

When you are habituated to this
It will not be difficult.
Your virtue will flourish organically.
It will make you wise
In all the things that you should understand.

So make an ever increasing study
Of a variety of methodologies and scriptural traditions.
Make observations and have discussions.
Let your heart flow with them.

Those who are wise in the classics,
And use discrimination regarding their details,
Are not totally confused regarding the application or rejection
Of things that must be retained or expunged.

To be specific,
When you attend to the magnificent ways of the holy Dharma,
Do not be satiated,
For they are the heart essence of the things that we must understand,
And they increase the virtue there is in our brilliant knowledge.

When our minds are apprehensive
It will remain difficult to help the people.
Just so, although we may have heard something,
It will be extremely difficult to do anything meaningful
When we are not sure what the meaning is.

So use the proper methodologies
To scrutinize anything you may hear,
And you will be sure about its meaning.
This is like putting our eyes on forms
While we illuminate them.

When we flow with this kind of attention and analysis
Our knowledge progressively grows,
Though it be bit by bit.
It is the same with bees and their honey.

This is a magnificent technique,
For it turns out to be an empowerment
Into the Dharma that has been transmitted.
It is like the harvest is for those who work in business,
And the Dharma that we understand
Is like a magnificent source of food.

These are the methods by which we may ascertain
The sorrows of the world,
That their causes are karma and emotional problems,
And so enhance our virtues.

We recollect on disgust,
On friendship,
On apportioning the domains of things that occur in dependencies,
And on the letting out and taking in of our breath.

We comprehend the discrepancies
In the things that we receive and those that we retain,
And keep them in balance.
And so we abide in the happiness there is in high status.

We travel on the road
Where accumulations and applications

Advice to Kublai Khan

Are for the world,
While seeing, meditation, and reaching the end,
Leave the world behind.

We use specific methods and studies
Which have been brilliantly categorized
By teachers, lineages of students,
And those whose virtues are pure,
To achieve nirvana.

This is only a summary discussion
Of the way of the Dharma
Belonging to the little vehicle.
It will serve as a ladder
For our climbing onto the great vehicle.

The opportunity to present the tradition of the little vehicle
Comes second.

This is how it is:
We strive toward our personal objectives,
With regard to both the present and the hereafter,
But we fail,
With regard to the magnificent methods
Which are the aims of other beings.
We therefore distance ourselves from Buddhahood.

One who perseveres toward the objectives of other beings
Will succeed at the important goals
That they and other beings aim toward.
How could it be possible
For someone who fails to help others,
Due to their own selfish objectives,
To consummate their own aims?

We may talk about this a lot,
But what will we get out of that?
There are kings who protect the kingdom,
And there are those who use their income and compensation
Only to protect themselves.
Look at the difference between the two.

We must achieve that omniscience
That comes from the oceanic practice
Of taking delight in the objectives of other beings,
Which is simply to be a companion for everyone that is alive.

To do this,
I beg you to receive the Victorious One,
The one who has achieved both his own aims and those of others,
The Great Vehicle,
The one that allows us to succeed at these things,
And the Sangha,
The one that does not turn back,
As holy refuges that you share in common with everyone alive,
Until you have understood these things,
For he is our teacher and he makes us happy,
For it is what we use to travel and what we depend on,
For they are our friends and they bring us together into a community.

They are, as it turns out,
The basis by which we actually achieve
The precious jewel of an enlightened attitude,
Which is the source of everything that we wish for,
And which outshines any other virtues there may be
In this world or in its pacification.

Our mind has no attributable source
Other than our mind.
We have no reason for our identity to have suddenly existed,
And there isn't one.

The reason that there are minds is that there is sentience.
So there does not exist, under any circumstance,
A delimitation on the beginning of our minds,
But because we have them,
We are sentient beings.

The sky is not delimited by a father.
The domain of the world is just the same.
You must know that the sentient beings that live in it
Are not quantified,
But are the objects of our friendship and our love.

By force of their individual karma,

Advice to Kublai Khan

They are everywhere tormented
By heaps of sorrow,
Which they do not want.

They perpetually spin on through their three pathways,
Like the circles made by burning torches
That are spun around in circles.
These are descriptive words for the world.

But while this is so,
Its domain is the natural reality
That is the embodiment of the Dharma.
If, therefore, we have the means,
All these things will turn out to be our Buddhahood.

But because our attunement and our inclinations are weak,
Because our conditions are despicable,
And because our friends are mean,
We fail to be of help to other beings.
We do not complete our own objectives, either.
So we move on,
Just to escape.
These are descriptive words for pacification.

The mightiest of sages has said
That these things are like cities built in the wilderness,
For their fruition is temporary.
They will, by degrees, be conquered.

Toward those who wish to dwell forever
In the world's happiness,
Or in that which transcends the world,
And would be joined with a stainless cause
For both life and death,
We are friendly.

Toward the sort that go after the sorrows of the world,
Or the denigrated vehicle and its fruits,
And wish to remove themselves from associations with a cause,
We are compassionate.

This is why I beg you to always be friendly and compassionate
Toward them.

But we may go on with an attitude of friendship and love,
While we fail to engage in any methods for these things,
Or we may engage in them,
Yet lack strength,
So we will not be of help to other beings.

This is why the perfect Buddha himself
Purged his problems,
And brilliantly discovered a holy force and power
To truly connect with every virtue,
So that he might consummate his knowledge and love.

He was also conscious of prayer, and prayed:
"I have come from being a sentient being,
So may I also be like them."
He relied on his companions in virtue,
And used a ritual with a full complement of subdivisions,
To make his vows like this.
He gave birth to an enlightened attitude that was prayerful.

An attitude of engagement is a longing that may be expressed like this:
"I will work to the end,
In every way and means there may be,
To achieve the success that is Buddhahood."
This is how he gave birth to an engaged attitude
Through taking a vow.

These are the methods whereby
Those who have not given birth to these things
May give birth to them,
And those who have given birth to them
May make them develop more fully.
We pray with great exuberance,
And consummate our engagement through exertion.

In their consideration of the way to practice prayer and engagement
Some of the Victorious One's children have used the example
That a prayer is just like a wish to go,
While engagement is like going.

But only a few of them use this method
To explain the difference between prayer and engagement
As they relate to our attitude,

Advice to Kublai Khan

Our giving birth to an attitude,
And our practice.

When we make a determination that
This is a relative enlightened attitude,
The real thing here is a plurality,
And is connected to what comes after it.
So it is not one thing.

When there is no unity,
How could there be a plurality?
And what could there be
That is neither of these two?
There is nothing like that that exists,
So we will be collecting non-entities.
This is a contradiction,
So it follows that both of these
Have no natural reality.

There is nothing that functions to prove this, either,
So it is not the case that both are non-existent,
And, on scrutiny, there is nothing that remains.

While our intellects cannot even hold on to a definition,
This is a sufficient causal source
For an enlightened attitude of holy significance.
This is a perspective that, in fact,
Continues to be superior in every circumstance.

We have no clinging,
So we keep things in balance.
We use similes,
And every validating principle,
For our ascertainments,
And so we immerse ourselves
In an enlightened attitude of holy significance.

We understand the grim prospects there are
In the world and in its pacification,
So we remove ourselves from longing for them.
We recollect the virtues of Buddhahood,
And constantly long for them.
We balance and interchange ourselves with other beings,

So we are exuberant about helping others.
We are neither dejected nor depressed,
So we embark onto the ways of engagement.
This is a prayerful attitude about enlightenment.
It is a magnificent method,
For it ensures that we make it to the end.

Practicing the accumulation of merit and wisdom
Ensures that we consummate our engagement.
To do this there are the six perfections,
Which ensure the completion of our Dharma of Buddhahood.
We are motivated by love.
We do not conceptualize the three involvements:
An actor, an object, and a thing.
We do not postpone and are not complacent.
We fulfill the hopes of our disciples entirely,
So they are united in enlightenment.
So it is that we ensure that everyone has it.

We long to get rid of our material things,
And have no fears regarding trifles.
Our Dharma is friendship.
We grant it in a way that is reasonable.
This is the perfection of giving.

We long to be rid of unmentionables,
And are exuberant about consolidating virtues.
We relinquish our faults and practice virtue.
We unite toward the objectives of other beings.
This is the perfection of the rule of the way.

We long to be rid of disruptions,
And do not consider intolerance of any kind.
Our minds are assured, so we are not disturbed.
This is the perfection of patience.

We are exuberant about bringing together virtues.
We don our armor and are not dejected.
We are not disturbed and are not complacent.
This is the perfection of diligence.

We long for our minds to be un-agitated,
And consolidate our minds with regard to all their objects.

Advice to Kublai Khan

We brilliantly settle our minds into our minds.
This is the perfection of dhyāna meditation.

We long to understand everything,
So we comprehend what is relatively real,
Then scrutinize it till we understand that it has no true reality.
This is the perfection of wisdom.

These are systematic remedies
For avarice, lecherous ways, wrath,
Laziness, confusion, and misunderstanding,
So they destroy all our faults.

As a whole, they make us wise in all things:
Possessions, happy living, good form,
The realization of all our objectives, and a peaceful mind.
They are the fruition of our temporary conditions.

The first five make our accumulations of merit
Grow constantly.
The sixth one, respectively, makes our accumulation of wisdom
Totally complete.
Furthermore, the five turn out to be Peaceful Abiding,
While the sixth turns out to be Higher Perception.
For it has been explained
That when our minds abide in peace
We will scrutinize things,
And perceive a higher objective.

The former of them will pacify our emotional problems,
And make pristine our samadhi and knowledge of what is real.
The latter will draw out all our faults,
And make pristine our knowledge and wisdom.

Both of them are based on the rule of the way.
The three latter ones are conditions for our success.

If we constantly scrutinize them,
Each one of them has six aspects and both parts.
It follows that we must know
That each of them is six fold,
And that each has two aspects,
So we must constantly immerse ourselves in them.

When we do this
Buddhahood is not far off.

There are four sorts of material things
That work in combination
Toward the maturation of sentient beings,
So we donate goods and services,
And make announcements to our disciples about it,
So that they may laugh in happiness during the current situation.

We speak pleasantly,
To explicate the Perfections correctly,
Just as they are,
So that those who practice these objectives
Will be truly united in the applications we present.
We get them to develop an enthusiasm for the meaning
By engaging them in objectives that accommodate our own.

Using the avenues of goods and services,
We use the Dharma to bring the first three together.
This also functions toward starting out helpfully.
The last three function toward liberation,
For all techniques toward helping others
Are subsumed within them.

In this way we gather the two accumulations
And brilliantly strive toward our two objectives,
But we use the way of illusion to do this,
Immersing ourselves in a yoga that we do not conceptualize.

The concern of the holy ones is enlightenment,
Which may be defined as the sky.
A mind that has no shadows
Will experience this directly.

We use the tree of life, which is expertise in methods,
To assemble a most excellent chariot,
One with the twin wheels of merit and wisdom.
It has a seat that is a vastness of commitment,
And has the features of recollection, diligence, and samadhi.

We use prayer as a driver.
We embark out on the paths

Advice to Kublai Khan

Where things accommodate freedom,
Using it to travel along the first, second, and third.

We get on this sort of magnificent chariot,
Holding to the five avenues of our strength,
And keep to the five avenues of our sensory perception.
We link it up with one or two elephants.
We move along the path
Where things accommodate our breakthrough into certainty.

Once we have truly set out,
We meet up with the magnificent ocean
Of the wisdom of the noble.
This is called the path of application.

As we travel along the stages of the path
We brilliantly evade the briars
Where the problems that have bogged down our vision
Accumulate,

And just as the luminescence of the sky
Falls upon the sea,
We see, by the ocean where the balance we keep in our minds
And the dominion of the Dharma,
Have the single taste of wisdom,
What we have not seen before:

A most excellent harbor that has seven features,
Avenues toward enlightenment that are precious.
We actually embark there.
This is called the path of seeing.

We climb onto the magnificent boat
Of a wisdom that is not conceptual.
It has a mast made of the branches of the Noble Path,
Finely ornamented with their eight features,

And through the blessings of the Victorious One
The winds of time accommodate our travels,
And we voyage on to the harbor of peace
In the dominion of the Dharma.

Our meditation resembles the waves upon the sea,
So we eschew all the problems that have bogged us down.
We become empowered into the precious jewels
Of the noble Dharma that we have studied.
We meditate on the meaning of what we see.
This is the path of meditation.

Once we have truly crossed over
The paths of this world and what is beyond it,
Which are like the earth and the sea,
We will seem to pass through a doorway
Into an island of wish fulfilling jewels.

We will have reached the end of the road we have travelled.
We will have overcome every quarter that was not accommodating.
We will have arrived at a wondrous end.
This is called the path where we reach the end.

The paths that are beyond the world
Are also divided into ten levels,
For just as the ocean,
Though it is the same as the water,
Appears to us differentially,
With reference to its foundation,
So too is liberation,
Which is the same as the Dharma,
Divided with reference to its foundation and its virtues.

When something serves to propagate our own virtues,
And supports the bounteous things that emerge from them,
It is a level.

The level of Total Delight nears us to Buddhahood.
It is where we embark upon the levels,
And delight in generosity.

The Filthless is where we are not stained
By the fault of hypocrisy in the rule of the way.

The Light Maker is where we maintain the vision
Of the transmitted Dharma,
And have the complexion of patience.

Advice to Kublai Khan

The Effulgent Light is where the Dharmas we have conceptualized
Are truly burned by fire,
And we blaze with diligence.

The Difficult Study is where we use the study of difficult things,
The study of alternatives,
And dhyāna meditation,
To protect our minds.

The level of Becoming Real is where we depend on wisdom
To see the Dharmas of samsara and nirvana directly.

Gone Far Away is where we use the finest methods,
Which are far beyond definition,
To be especially noble.

The level of The Unshakable is where we are not harassed
By any conceptual constructs,
And we abide well with prayer.

The Mind of the Good is where we use the majestic power
Of four correct understandings
To teach the Dharma.

The Cloud of Dharma is where the clouds that hold our samadhi
Condense within the sky of wisdom.

In the end,
The Vajra Samadhi opens the mouth of a jeweled treasure,
And by its power our four stations are transformed
Into wonders that our thoughts cannot comprehend.

We achieve that Buddhahood
That is the sole companion of all sentient beings.
We relinquish all the filth that has shadowed us,
As if it were battalions of clouds
Vanishing in the sky,
And our dominion and our wisdom
Come to have a single taste.
This is described as our embodiment in natural reality.

Through the force of innumerable methods
And our compassion,
We enjoy the fields, teachers, retinues, and times,
The Dharma that is sure, and a magnificent bliss.
This is our embodiment in perfect pleasure.
It has thirty-two wondrous qualities,
For we will have parted from our personal objectives.

The power to know where to stay and where not to stay,
Knowledge of the domains of karma,
And of the senses,
Reverence,
The motion of all things,
Laughter,
Continuing to rejoice,
Memories on the trail,
Transference at death,
And the dissipation of impurities.
These are the ten powers of a sage.

We overcome the shadows,
Demonic mandalas,
And ancestral disputes,
Which makes us the equal of a vajra.

We have no fear at all
About correctly teaching relinquishment and wisdom,
The path of renunciation and the things that obstruct it,
Just as they are.
These are the four kinds of fearlessness.

We are like the lions,
Arrogant in style,
For we protect the people that we must train,
And help them to leave behind their disputes.

To be without delusion or babble,
To keep things in balance
Without being forgetful.
To relinquish discriminatory opinions,
To be rid of equanimities that are not applicable,
To be rid of failings
In our wishes,

Advice to Kublai Khan

Our diligence,
Our recollection,
And our wisdom,
To be rid of total failure
In our freedom,
And in the wisdom to be free,
To follow on the trails of wisdom
With regard to our actions,
Be they physical, verbal, or mental,
To apply a vision of unshadowed wisdom
Through the past to the future,
And in the present:
These are the unadulterated Dharmas of a sage.
There are eighteen of them.

They cover everything,
And nothing covers them,
Just like the sky.
If we were to here parcel out the wondrous virtues
That are distinct from these,
They would be beyond reckoning.
You must understand that alternative presentations,
Such as the Ten Powers,
Are subsumed within this one.

The Buddha's body has thirty two wondrous aspects
By which his altruistic intentions are brought to maturity.
His feet are level,
They are marked with wheels,
The heels are wide,
And the toes are long,
They are connected by webs,
And their flesh is youthful,
Their forward span has the radiance of a stag.
His privates are drawn inward,
And have a lion's mantle.
His palms are very wide.
His knees are rounded.
His arms are long.
His body is the finest, for it is clean.
His neck is flawless, like a conch.
He has the cheeks of a lion.
He has forty teeth.

Their texture is fine and even.
The canines are white.
His tongue is long,
It has the finest sense of taste,
And the cadence of a *kalapinga* bird.
His eyes are the best, dark blue.
His eyebrows are thick.
The spot of hair between his eyebrows is brilliantly white.
His hair-knot is so high
That we cannot see it when we look.
His skin is smooth.
It has a golden hue.
Each of his body hairs spouts out clockwise.
The hair on his head is like a dark blue sapphire.
He is symmetrical, like a nyagrodha Bodhi tree.
His body is the best,
For it has great strength.
These are the thirty-two marks.

The things described as the eighty exemplary features
Are subdivisions of these.
These are the glories of his physical embodiment.

When the autumn is in its fullness of luster,
And the mandala of the moon is in the fullness of its perfection,
It resembles a boot
That climbs the ranges of the moving stars,
And when this same boot,
There in the midst of the moving stars,
Dawns upon the water of a lake,
The children are filled with joy.

So it is that when we store up accommodating virtues,
We will perceive things in an accommodating way,
And we will achieve our objectives.
This is described in keeping with the Mahayana Upadeśa Sutra.

This embodiment of perfect pleasure
Is a force of merit for innumerable living things,
And it appears to us in a variety of ways
To fulfill our objectives.
These are the Buddha's manifest embodiments.

Advice to Kublai Khan

His natural embodiment constitutes
That most excellent wisdom
That regards the dominion of the Dharma.
The Buddha's perfect pleasure
Is none other than the wisdom of the mirror.
His equanimity and comprehension of particulars
Are simply specializations of this.
The wisdom to get things done
Coordinates the Buddha's manifestations harmoniously.

Now these embodiments and wisdoms
Are respectively classified
As supports and what is supported,
As personal objectives and altruistic objectives,
And as being subtle or coarse.

The river of Buddhahood is never dammed,
For its flavor is identical to its inexhaustible domain,
For it is born out of an inexhaustible cause,
For it overcomes every position of discord,
For it truly makes our prayers come true,
For it reveals empowerment and endowment in all things,
For the objectives of its projects never run out.
And so it is that its teachings
Abide forever throughout the dominions of the world.
They do not appear and disappear.

Things that we see rise and fall,
That flourish and then fail,
Are the conceptual constructs of living beings.
They appear by the power of karma,
Not by the force of their objective positions.

It seems like the sky appears and disappears,
And that the sun rises and sets,
But that is not how it is.
It is the same with regard to the pure yogas,
For they are forever blessed by the Victorious Ones,
And are perpetually practiced
At the delightful parties of the holy Dharma.
This is amazing.
It's a miracle.

Chogyal Phagpa

This has been a mere summary discussion
Of the Mahayana Dharma.
You will learn of its vastness elsewhere.

If we properly employ the traditions of our human Dharmas
Toward these magnificent objectives,
Than which there are no higher,
It will not be long
Till we travel throughout the nations of the gods.

When we climb the ladders of gods and humans
Our freedom is right up ahead.
When we use the three vehicles to reach certitude
We will maintain that freedom that is our sole vehicle.
So it has been proclaimed,
For the stages of our objectives are like this,
And so I have described them here.

The communities of those who observe the other side
Are extremely wise,
And they have already elucidated
Their multitudinous enumerations of the way of the Dharma,
Over and over.

This is surely so,
But in my effort to comprehensively instruct your very heart,
And so that this may be of help to others,
I have been brief and clear.

I have, nonetheless, spoken out,
Even though the disposition of my intellect is childish,
And I have not yet studied exhaustively the things that we must know.
I have, as well, composed this in haste.

May those of great intelligence
Be forever patient
When they receive this.

Through the virtue there is in it,
May everyone alive make good use of it,
In the way of the world.
May they enter through the portals of the ambrosial holy Dharma,
And may we all become true Buddhas.

This Rosary of Gemstones: A Discourse for Prince Jibig Timur was composed by Phagpa in the year of the male fire tiger (1266/67 A.D.), on the eighth day of the month of the bangle, at the magnificent Dharma School of Glorious Sakya. There are two hundred and four verses.

Chogyal Phagpa

THE STAGES OF PRACTICE
IN BRILLIANT CLARITY:
WRITTEN FOR DUCHESS PUNDARI

dPon mo pundari'i don du mdzad pa bsgrub pa'i rim pa rab tu gsal ba

I bow at the feet of my holy guru.

No matter what sorrow or happiness may come to us on account of external and internal conditions, we must not be depressed or joyous about them. They occur through the karma of our previous actions. These sorrows and happinesses will also change and end. So look at it like this: When we have illness, the sorrows of parting from beloved friends, the theft of our possessions, when we are ridiculed by others and they say unpleasant things, we must not get stuck in the sorrow and become depressed, saying: "It isn't right that these things happen to me."

These sorts of experiences that are difficult to bear do not occur on account of extenuating conditions in our present life. In previous lifetimes we did the evils that are the cause for it to happen that we experience these kinds of things.

Specifically, it is because we have brought others to sorrow and created conditions for other beings to have unhappy minds that we too will experience these kinds of sorrows. In the Blessed One's Sutra Literature it is proclaimed:

> The Karma of embodied beings
> Will not be exhausted in a hundred eons,
> But will ripen in its own fruition.

When the karmic conditions of our own actions are complete, they ripen unto us. So who is there to retaliate on?

To be specific, when we do harm to others, it turns out that we are doing harm to ourselves. This is reality. Engaging in the Practice[7] says:

In my past,
I did harm sentient beings in these ways.
It is correct that these things happen to me,
For I have harmed sentient beings.

We think about the meaning of this proclamation, and we repeatedly bring to mind that all the damage and sorrow that have come about are our own faults, and that through experiencing these kinds of sorrow the evils of the past will be cleansed, which is good. Through our own experience of the fruition of evil in these ways, the bad karma that every sentient being has gathered, through any act of evil, must also be cleansed.

When the conditions we set up through our own bad karma from the past make every sentient being experience karmas of sorrow, we get additional bad karma, and when we do things that are harmful to others we will have immeasurable sorrows in the future. So we take a vow:

From now on,
Even if I lay down my life,
I will not do evil in general,
And specifically, I will not harm others.

To be specific, the Prince, who was like a Bodhisattva, has passed into his peace, and this has become a heart-wrenching situation for you. You must remember the way it is with these things. You have had an extremely profound and especially noble connection with his father, mother, and staff. You have performed services for his ancestors and helped sentient beings in many ways. These are extraordinary deeds.

This has not come about through the force of luck in this lifetime alone. In the past you created vast roots of merit in common with them, and you made a special prayer in your hearts that you would join with each other, as so it came to pass.

However, this was accomplished through vast roots of merit that were only temporary, and they did not make it to the end. So for only the smallest of reasons you have been split from each other.

Whether this is due to your virtues having run out, or that you were a couple united for a special purpose, or that the opinions of many men had

---

[7] sPyod 'jug

been rejected and so they created an obstruction to your virtue, or that while you were living according to the Dharma your exceptional accord had been disrupted, it has come to pass that you are experiencing the sorrow of being separated before the time was right. The experience of these kinds of sorrows is difficult to bear. They turn into causes by which we do harm to ourselves by the things that we do. We put the blame on everyone else.

You have experienced all these undesirable sorrows due to the bad karma you have gathered from before and from everything you are doing to find fault with others. Be done with it! Be at peace! Let the power of this experience bring peace to the evil deeds and bad karma of all sentient beings!

I beg you to meditate in your thinking that you are standing before a special domain and use your mind to visualize this right before you. By doing only this, your obstructions from the past will be cleansed and they will no longer, for one or two lifetimes at least, obstruct you.

It will not be too long before the two of you will be born together in an exceptionally wonderful environment. Your connections in the world and in the Dharma will grow deeper as you join. You will live together for an extremely long time. You will enjoy the happiness you have from the Dharma and from the things you own equally, and you will work toward success in the teachings and toward a great vastness of objectives for the sake of sentient beings.

Right now you must truly comprehend the stages and the paths, for this will comfort you. To do this, make offerings to the Precious Jewels, offer services for the Sangha, erect shrines for the Precious Jewels and build libraries. Endow them as foundations to provide support for the Sangha in the four directions. Requisition the necessities for continuous offerings during special times. Donate generously for the impoverished and the ill. Moreover, engage yourself joyously in any yoga practice with a Yidam you may prefer, under every circumstance.

When you do these things you must repeatedly dedicate what you do, saying:

May the Prince that I and my kin revere, who is known by his name, attain the status of a god or a human and be endowed with the seven wondrous virtues in all the successions of his lifetimes, and may we have memories of our lifetimes in the past, and bring things together into situations where all the roots of merit that we share with each other are consummated. When this happens, may no harm be done, externally or internally. May we achieve every objective we think upon, in keeping with the Dharma. Through bringing the roots of virtue that we share to full completion, may we at last reach unexcelled and completely perfect enlightenment.

You will succeed in your purpose, no matter what happens.

The Sutra on Mañjuśrī's Arrangement of the Buddha Fields[8] proclaims:

All Dharmas accord with their conditions,
So consecrate them in your unions at the roots.
Whatever prayer you present
Will bring a fruition of its kind.

In the past, at the time that Śākyamuṇi became a Bodhisattva, when he was the son of a Brahmin by the name of Star, the daughter of a businessman who had a perfect store of heritage and physique fell in love with him. She asked him to marry her. So this son of a Brahmin named Star felt compassion for her, and gave up his celibate life. They got married, and they did not obstruct each other's virtues. They took a vow that they would be friends in enlightenment. They reconciled what they had collected over many eons, and from that day forth they remained married without being separated throughout all their rebirths and lifetimes. In the end, that son of a Brahmin Star became the Buddha Śākyamuṇi. The daughter of a businessman became Yaśodharā.

These things are proclaimed in the Sutra on Skill in the Methods of Great Secrecy[9] and other sources, for they are spoken of in many of the Sutras.

This being so, at first you may have temporal burdens, and it will be difficult to get a chance to meet, but after a while you will meet forever. You have reasons to remember each other through the successions of your lives, so you will recognize each other, and you will be friends toward the total perfection of each other's roots of virtue. To make this happen, do not act miserable and tormented, for it is appropriate for you to persevere toward the success of your ultimate and vast purpose. I have condensed this from the contents of the Profound Sutra on Upadeśa for Taking Sorrow on the Path.[10]

Moreover, look at it like this: You have a body and youth, a perfect store of power, friends and a child, and a consummate retinue. You have acquired the most luxurious possessions. Your fame is renowned. You have attained a perfect store of power and wealth. You must, however, dedicate these things, saying:

"My acquisition of a perfect store of wealth and glory did not come

---

[8] 'Jam dpal gyi sangs rgyas kyi zhing bkod pai mdo
[9] gSang chen thabs la mkhas pa'i mdo
[10] sDug bsngal lam du bslang pa'i man ngag zab mo'i mdo

about through some extenuating circumstance of my life. In my previous lifetimes, in very special lands, I gathered up roots of virtue in abundance, and worked on these roots of virtue with my body and speech, as well as my mind. So it is that I now am endowed with such luxuries. These things were made up out of virtuous causes from the past, and when the river of virtue from what I have done before runs dry, my perfect store of possessions will be exhausted and destroyed, like oil lamps going out when the oil is finished. These possessions of mine will come to nothing, or they will meet with disagreeable circumstances, and become a basis for disputes. It is possible that they once again become causes for evil.

The Sutras proclaim:

Wealth is at the root of all acquisition and loss.

The Master Nagarjuna said:

There are cases in which lords of the earth
With great virtues from of yore
Were later born into horrible lives.

Master Metrīpa said:

On account of goods and services
There will be disputes.
When we own no goods or services
Our happiness is the best.

You must recollect the meaning of such proclamations. Do not be attached to or arrogant about your temporary possessions. These things were made out of roots of virtue from the past. You need to acquire happiness and possessions for the future. Once you get thinking about this, you must work toward roots of virtue.

From among your possessions you should give a part as offerings to the Precious Jewels, a portion to support the Sangha and to distribute charity to the ill, a portion for the common people, which should be distributed at holidays, and you must introduce your dear kin, your close friends, and your retinue to the Dharma. Encourage them toward roots of merit, and make a dedication that through these roots of merit, may we ultimately attain the status of Buddhahood, and for the duration till we attain it may we acquire the perfect stores of the endowments of humans and gods.

Repeatedly do these sorts of things. Your roots of virtue from the past and roots of virtue in the future will be joined together, and you will enjoy an undammed river of the happiness of gods and humans, without the sorrows of horrible lives or the disadvantages there are in high status. Ultimately, in unsurpassed completely perfect enlightenment, you will truly become a Buddha.

Once in the past there was an impoverished man who offered a load of flowers to a Buddha, and asked to develop an enlightened attitude. He dedicated himself to enlightenment, and through all his lifetimes he did not fall into a horrible life, but enjoyed the happiness of high status. In this very eon he got the name of a Buddha, and has come to be known as the Tathagata King of the Power and Wealth of Flowers. This is proclaimed in the Fortunate Eon Sutras:[11]

> One who brilliantly offers a single flower
> Will not fall into a horrible life,
> At a specific time it will be shown
> That his name resembles what he did before.

This exemplifies how all our happiness, goodness, and joy have come forth from our previous virtues, and these were based on the Precious Jewels. They are the kindnesses of the Precious Jewels.

This is how we must recollect the kindness of the Precious Jewels. We must also continue to acquire all the happiness there is in this world and in the beyond by relying on our guru and the Precious Jewels.

To do this, we go for refuge from the bottoms of our hearts to our guru and the Precious Jewels. We must remember to present our requests in our thoughts. When we see or hear of the perfect glories and endowments that others have, their joys, happinesses, and possessions, we do not meditate on being jealous about these things. They have worked on roots of virtue, so we must rejoice that they have come to possess these sorts of perfect accumulations.

Moreover, what would be wrong about it if these people, and all other sentient beings, also enjoyed vast roots of virtue? We must rejoice in our thoughts. This is a special Dharma for taking happiness on the path. I am talking about things that are found in the Sutras.

Now transforming any happiness or sorrow there may be into a path, using our skills in Bodhisattva methods, is discussed extensively in the Sutra literature for Bodhisattvas. The Ornament of the Sutras by Lord Maitreya proclaims:

> All these Dharmas are like illusions.
> When men and women understand
> That they seem to be going to pieces,

---

[11] mDo sde bskal ba bzang po

Then when they are acquiring things,
Or even when their things are being stolen,
They have no fear for the sorrows of emotional problems.

The meaning of this proclamation has been organized into a progressive practice of bringing it into our own experience.

Likewise, when we give birth to conceptualizations that are desirous, hateful, or stupid, we examine them well and investigate all of them. What are the objects we develop emotional problems over? What kind of attitude do these emotional problems develop? Just how do these emotional problems develop? When we understand that these emotional problems are, in their essence, empty, the emotional problems stop, and we embark onto the way of the Dharma of emptiness. After this has come about, we contemplate mentally and also must say: "May the emotional problems of all sentient beings also be eliminated this way, and may they enter the samadhi of the door of emptiness." These are the upadeśa for taking emotional problems on the path. Lord Maitreya's Ornament of the Sutras proclaims:

There are no Dharmas
That are not connected to the dominion of the Dharma,
For any reason.
This is why the Buddhas consider there to be
Repulsion, attachment, and other sentiments
Toward them.

These are the upadeśa for bringing the meaning of what I mentioned above into your experience.

Furthermore, when we are enjoying attractive forms, sounds, smells, tastes, and tangibles, we enjoy them while thinking that anything that may happen to be an object of our desires transforms immeasurably, seeming to be a cloud of offerings for the All Good. We think of ourselves as being Buddhas, and we offer it to all the Buddhas of the ten directions. All of them are pleased, and they give us their blessings. Then we imagine that all sentient beings are satiated by the happiness there is in the things we desire. We also do not become addicted or attached to these things. We must understand that they have no true nature. On this, the Tantra for Cleansing Horrible Lives proclaims:

After seating ourselves in the place of Vajrasattva,
We eat everything,
And do everything,
But we are not stained with any problems that might develop,

And we maintain our compassion, as if it need be mentioned.

This is the meaning of the upadeśa for transforming the enjoyment of the happiness in the things we desire into a path.

Moreover, when we lie down on the mattress at night, we say: "May I reach the vajra throne at the heart of enlightenment."

When we clamp on our belts and our sashes, we say: "May I connect the ends of methods and wisdom."

When we are taking a bath, we say: "May the obstructions I have due to emotional problems and the things that I must know be cleansed."

When we are putting on jewelry, we say: "May the jewels of the Tathagata's wonders make me beautiful."

When we eat food, we say: "May I eat the food of inexhaustible samadhi."

When we are going outside, we say: "May I go outside from samsara."

When we go on a pathway, we say: "May I go on the path to enlightenment."

When we are crossing over waters, we say: "May I cross over the rivers of sorrow."

When we are climbing a ladder, we say: "May I climb the ladder of freedom."

When we meet up with people, we say: "May I meet up with noble people."

When we see an empty vessel, we say: "May I be empty of faults."

When we see a full vessel, we say: "May I be full with wonders."

When we see or hear the Dharma being explained, we say: "May I see and hear the Tathagata turning the wheel of the Dharma."

When we are kicking out vicious people and terminating their activities, we say: "May I overcome Mara and his reverted deliverance."

When we are distributing aid to those who live in misery, we say: "May all sentient beings be granted the breath of the Dharma."

When we open the door of a house, we say: "May I open the door to nirvana."

When we enter a house, we say: "May I enter the city of great freedom."

When we are eating, drinking, or enjoying a party with others, we say: "May I take pleasure in the happiness of the Dharma with all sentient beings."

When we converse back and forth and we are talking and listening, we say: "Through talking about the Dharma, may my mind, and the minds of others, be happy."

When we open doors, just as before, and close them behind us, we say: "May I work toward the objectives of sentient beings."

At any time it may be appropriate we use ways such as those mentioned above for everything we do, entering a house and all the rest.

When we distribute any gifts, great or small, we say: "Through the karma of my giving, may all sentient beings be perfect in the perfection of giving, and may we become Buddhas."

When we make the rule of the way real, beginning with a single day of fasting, or do things to guard that portion, we say: "Through the karma of my keeping the rule of the way, may all sentient beings perfect the perfection of the rule of the way, and become Buddhas."

When we are harmed by others and their reverted practices, but our minds bear the pain, when we are engaged in difficult practices, but tolerate the difficulty, and when we meditate on patient understanding, we say: "Through the karma of my patience, may I and all sentient beings be perfect in our perfection of patience, and become Buddhas."

When we engage diligently with our bodies, speech, and minds toward any roots of virtue that may be fitting, we say: "Through the karma of my diligence, may I and all sentient beings perfect the perfection of diligence, and become Buddhas."

When we are meditating on friendship, compassion, or an enlightened attitude, and when we settle into equanimity with a visualization of a god or some other, we say: "Through the karma of my dhyāna meditation, may I and all sentient beings perfect the perfection of dhyāna, and become Buddhas."

When we listen to the Dharma, inquire into it, see it, scrutinize its intent, and when we propagate wisdom, working things out in our minds according to the Dharma in general and our own characteristics, we say: "Through the karma of my wisdom, may I and all sentient beings perfect the perfection of wisdom, and become Buddhas."

This technique is described by the forever young Mañjuśrī in the Buddha's Avatamsaka. He calls them: "Entirely pure practice fields."

On this same point, lord Maitreya proclaims in his Ornament of the Sutras:

> While you enjoy being a prince,
> You must be aware of just how to make
> Your senses engage in a multitude of practice fields,
> And use appropriate words to make it real,
> So that you may help sentient beings.

We must take the significance of this into our experience. These are the upadeśa for transforming everything we usually do into a path.

This has been a representation of the path that uses skill in methods for transforming our happiness and sorrow, everything that is outside or inside us, into a path toward enlightenment.

Now I will talk about the way that everything we do is shared by both the Dharma and the world:

You have an inspiration that is difficult for ordinary people to fathom. Everything you do through your three doors, body, speech and mind, is attractive. People are happy to befriend you. Due to the luster of your honest comportment none of these people are able to engage in deceitful practices. You overwhelm them by your very character.

Be stable in your heart's intuition and in everything you do, and have nothing to do with intrigue. Master Nagarjuna was talking about this in his Rosary of Precious Jewels:

> Be deep like the ocean.
> Be present like a full moon.
> Be glowing like the autumn moon.
> Be very stable like Mt. Meru.

When you understand what this means you will live in a happy understanding. If you do your work in keeping with this technique, your work will be pure. If you internalize it, it will bring you the knowledge of omniscience.

> So I have explained the way of the Dharma according to tradition.
> Through any vast virtues that may be born from this
> May I and all sentient beings,
> The one who requests this being foremost,
> Practice in the way of the Dharma,
> And attain the holy station of Buddhahood.

This way of the Dharma called: "The Stages of Practice in Brilliant Clarity," was commissioned from afar by the Duchess named Pundari, who said: "Please write on a Dharma that will be of help to sentient beings," and sent consummately vast offerings. I, the monk Phagpa, composed it in the male iron dragon year (1280/81 A.D.), on the fifteenth day of the midmonth of autumn, during daytime, at the great Dharma school of glorious Sakya.

Advice to Kublai Khan

A BRILLIANT LETTER TO PRINCE NOMO KHAN: ONE HUNDRED AND EIGHT VERSES

rGyal bu no mo gan la spring ba'i rab byed

I bow to all the Buddhas and Bodhisattvas.

I bow to the lord of sages,
Who works with every way and tradition,
Towards true highness and sure goodness,
And is the glory of this world and its peace.

I have not been commissioned,
But my mind flows toward you and falls on you,
So while I would rather be commissioned,
What am I to do?
I am sending this letter to you.

All of these consummate stores that you have acquired by force
Were not given to you by some true essence,
Or by the sky,
Or by a god.
You were brought up by the power of the virtues
You performed in you previous lifetimes,
And your father, mother, and grandmothers
Worked to help you.

Therefore take joy in virtue and refresh your memory
About what your father, mother, and friends

Have done for you.
Endeavor to repay their kindness.

When there are gatherings
Among such folk as those who maintain austerities,
Those who maintain reason and virtue,
Or even when they are alone,
You must have respect and serve them.

Use your love to protect the miserable:
Those with no protector, the sick, those who are suddenly wiped out,
The aged, and those whose memories are failing,
Knowledgeable people who are impoverished,
Polite people who are disadvantaged,
And even those who have fallen into bad ways.
Do not denigrate them, but work to help them.

As for those who are wicked and concoct their poisons
While they practice trickery and deceit,
Turn them away from these ways,
Or dispatch them to somewhere far away.

As for those who employ themselves in awareness,
Who strive to help others,
And who properly support the way of honesty,
While they may live far away, you must draw them in.

The laws that were drawn up by the kings of yore
Certainly are old and antiquated,
But you must make them prosper everywhere
For they disallow doing damage to those who live,
And they function to help.

If you are overly exacting
Towards those who have taken oaths to the law,
The people will be heavily tormented,
And their oaths will quickly be broken.

The oaths of long long ago,
Are demeaned by the newest of the new.
Do not inquire into what your subjects are doing.
This will make their oaths be truly firm.

Advice to Kublai Khan

The objectives of ordinances
Will not fail completely
If their immediate concern
Is to do much for the sake of a few,
Or to do great things for the sake of the small.

The great say things into your ears:
Do this! These sorts of objectives will be achieved through this!
These are mostly things that fulfill their own objectives,
So you must scrutinize them in detail.

If you constantly round people up and gather taxes,
And have too many gatherings for this,
It will be like a cow that is milked too much.
You must worry about whether it will go dry.

As it is with the honey made by the bees,
If you gather a bit at the right time,
And don't waste it when you have gathered it,
Your acquisition will be in a good way.

When a poison snake looks at a man
It does not love him,
And is not skillful in its methods,
So it truly harms the other beings that it looks at.
To requisition things in this way is highly contemptible.

When you truly contemplate helping your subjects,
As you do your children,
Then they will honor you with respect,
Just as a son does for his father.

Through giving we follow the trail of virtue,
And so we find happiness in other worlds,
Our works are associated with happiness,
And we propagate joy in them.

Therefore, at all times
I beg you to plant in excess,
The seeds that accord with your needs,
In the fields of merit,
And in the fields of the lowly.

You will know the times and situations
That you and others may enjoy the many delights
Possessed by the harmless and augmented in their glory,
For this is the way of the gods.

You will understand that to enjoy these pleasures perversely,
Or not to enjoy them and let them go to waste,
Is wrong and meaningless,
And you will reject these ways.

The three causes for the depletion of merit
Are to be excessive in receiving amenities,
To enjoy things without being satisfied,
And to despise the glory of others.

The three causes for failure in our works
Are to savor the taste of bliss in our sleeping,
To depend on slothful habits,
And to take joy in idle talk.

The three causes that propagate illness
Are to be totally obsessed with coitus,
To be attached to the taste of beer,
And to be heedless in our behavior.

The three causes that diminish our lives
Are the putting to death of sentient beings
Who have done nothing wrong,
The scorning of non-human beings,
And the discontinuation of holiday rituals.

The three causes for failure in the way
Are to fail to serve those who are worthy of worship,
To compete against those who have failed,
And to have contempt for the lowly.

Once you understand that this is the way it is with these things,
I beg you to personally turn away from them,
And also to divert others from them.
Through this, your own glories will grow.

You will achieve your purposes.
You will live in happiness.

Advice to Kublai Khan

Your life-span will increase.
You will act according to the way.
This will make you, yourself,
And others happy.

When you do things well, the work is a joy,
And when you discontinue mistaken practices
In organizing your government and subjects
You will certainly be keeping to
The traditions of the protectors of the earth.

But if we scrutinize these traditions well,
They are used to accommodate the things we like to do,
Even when they are to be ridiculed,
And we eliminate the thoughts of others,
Which we do not tolerate.

We eliminate them,
But just as we consider leeching for someone who is sick,
Which is reasonable,
As it does reduce the illness,
But also resembles killing someone
To eliminate their illness,
Even though we do not take their lives.

People who have bad dispositions
Start out by doing good,
But they don't get too much high praise,
So they go on to do other things that cause harm.

Those who are naturally good,
Due to the influences of conditions,
Start out doing things mistakenly,
Yet people who try to stop them do not succeed,
For they are not overly blameworthy,
And their dispositions are so.

The common people make a living
On things like grass and water.
They live without doing harm.
But in their effort to eat birds and deer,
They harm them for the sake of amusement.
This is certainly present in the traditions of the ancients.

But when you clear your mind,
Through scrutinizing what is reasonable and what is not,
You will support ways that are reasonable,
So please scrutinize what is actually correct.

I personally live happily,
Using grains and fruits of various sorts,
Along with things like milk, yogurt, and salt,
And a variety of foods and drinks,
But would it be reasonable
If I destroyed my own happiness,
By using the hard work of the many,
In all its varieties,
To develop on my own evils and sorrows,
And to harm others?

To do these things would be to throw my life away.
They would harm my body,
And be painful.
This is an analogy,
For how I think of myself.

While they are frightened and terrified
Of such things as having their hands cut off by weapons,
The people around you have no place to flee.
They clunk around with hurried steps,
Because they are frightened.

Looking at it with intelligence,
You do not love these situations.
Do you have no compassion?
If you have it, I beg that you speak out
About your involvement in these things.

But it may be that for the sake of keeping tradition
You do not totally discontinue this.
Still, there are things that must be stopped.
Why don't you do this, for just these things?

The people of the world and the scriptures
Forbid ridicule and spite.
I beg you to accept as pure and promulgate

Advice to Kublai Khan

The things that are praised and are beneficial.

To sum it up,
I beg you to do only such things that
Augment your glory,
Do no harm to the glory of others,
And use glory as a cause for glory.

The fruition of this tradition
Is that your government and subjects will be happy,
That their happiness be transmitted as a river,
And that your own lineal transmission will be stable.

Paldrin[12] and the self-arising Jugse,[13]
The divine guru Yisuptsen,[14]
And the godless guru Bodrok[15],
And other such,
Are famed as the greatest of the great.

The works of Kapila, Kanada, Aksapada, and Ugdruk[16]
Were written by clear minded people.
The scriptures that were authored by backward thinkers,
Such as Lab gin, Mishaha, and Mahamed,
All deviate into the two extremes.
They are harmful to ourselves and others
In both their reality and their transmission,
And hence are only causes for the world and for horrible lives.

You are one with a shining wisdom,
So once you understand this clearly,
I beg you to reject them.

They have fine words with evil intentions,
Like poison that tastes delicious.
They encourage delight temporarily,
But later on they are only sources of sorrow.

---

[12] dPal mgrin
[13] Jug sred
[14] Yid srubs rtsen
[15] 'Bod sgrogs
[16] 'Ug phrug

Internally, they are not at peace,
Even though they do demonstrate good general behaviors,
Yet they cannot accommodate a stable mind.
They are like ducks and cats.

They do make a temporary peace,
But they fail to cut off the roots of this world,
As they do not have an ascertained disgust for it,
Which resembles using cold water in the progress toward warmth.

It follows that only the Sugata speaks out
On revulsion toward this world,
And the attainment of holy freedom.

He too sought out virtuous companions,
And used their compilations on the rule of the way
To control his body.
He listened to many, making his speech very pure.
He purified his heart with samadhi.
He was a companion who cared for sentient beings out of love,
The holiest of companions.

Anyone there may be who is like this
Is just like the Buddha himself.
We must support them with the highest respect.
We must learn from them the eight branches of fasting,
And keep to them.
By doing only this
We will attain the glory of our chosen deity.
That is what the Victorious One said.

Furthermore, when you practice your austerities,
Which you have vowed to do for your personal freedom,
It makes you beautiful,
For they are the foundation of every path.

But you will not attain great freedom
Except by the great vehicle.
You must totally let your heart flow
Into the great vehicle,
And you must immerse yourself in it.

Advice to Kublai Khan

Now any place that deceives you
When you take shelter there
Is not a place of refuge.
When it comes to the great beings
Who are gods and elemental spirits,
We only make offerings to them,
While we brilliantly flow into the true peace
Of such beings as the noble and those who are victorious by themselves.
It is worth it to bow down to them.
We may also go to them for a temporary refuge,
And thereby never move toward the problems
That we are habituated to.

The Sage alone is a wondrous treasure that never fails,
So he is the supreme refuge.

We must acquire the good proclamations
Of a supreme refuge like this,
And attain his status,
So we must travel along his way,
For it is truly our refuge.

Those who embark upon this trail
Will truly cascade into the ocean of its wisdom,
And so the Sangha of Bodhisattvas
Is a temporary refuge while we are students.

The refuge that we take in them
Must be taken on correctly,
And occurs to us through signs.
Once we have found this
There is no past and there is no future.

This is why we, along with all sentient beings,
Go for refuge to our companions in virtue,
Until we get to the heart-essence of enlightenment.
It is so that we may attain it.

Then we rely on excellent people,
And listen to the holy Dharma from them,
Practicing according to what we hear.
These are the three common trainings.

We do not accept in any way
Teachers who are not Buddhas,
Paths that are not the Dharma,
Or best friends who are not of the Sangha.

We study these, as the three parts of our personal training,
Everywhere and in all things.
When we are in pain,
We pray that we ourselves and others
Will be free of such things.
When we experience happiness
We recall that it is truly the kindness of the precious ones.

When we know that we are not separate
From the Buddha's embodiment as the Dharma,
Or the holy profundities of the Dharma's meaning,
Which is the Dharma that the Sangha works on,
And even a hundred ten millions of demons
Could not part them from the Buddha, Dharma, and Sangha:
That will be the time that we go for refuge.
We attain refuge through its reality.

This sort of going for refuge
Is the foundation of all virtues,
With no exceptions.

Once we have correctly taken up these refuges,
We must engender an enlightened attitude.
This attitude is subsumed into two types:
The relative and the ultimate.

The relative enlightened attitude is of two kinds:
Prayerful and engaged.

We take a vow before an object in a ritual
That we will attain our prayer and desire:
An enlightenment that is perfect in its work to help sentient beings.
This is how we engender a prayerful attitude.

When we take vows toward an attitude that is engaged,
Which is a desire to accomplish all the ways and means there are
To achieve Buddhahood,
We are engendering an engaged attitude.

Advice to Kublai Khan

We get rid of three attitudes:
Laziness, sloth, and fear of samsara's problems,
Then we meditate on five things:
Friendliness and compassion toward the living,
The horrible prospects there are in both the world and its pacification,
And a recollection of the virtues of Buddhahood.
We must guard our prayer for enlightenment
By truly supporting our good friends.

To deceive those who are worthy of offerings,
To be regretful about things that don't matter,
To cast blame on the finest of sentient beings,
And to behave with deceit and trickery:
These have been proclaimed to be the four Dharmas of darkness,
And are to be rejected in every way.

To speak the truth and be reasonable,
To be without guile and have an attitude of helping others,
To serve the children of the Victorious One and praise them,
And to join our minds with the great vehicle:
These have been proclaimed to be the four Dharmas of the light,
And we must fully immerse ourselves in them through everything.

To praise ourselves and ridicule others
Out of a desire for fame and services,
To refuse, out of avarice, to give the jewels of the Dharma
To those who are suffering and have no protector,
To refuse to listen to the confessions of others
And to strike them out of wrath,
To make them reject the Mahayana
And to teach a similitude of the holy Dharma:
These have been proclaimed to be root downfalls.
We must turn away from these activities.

To offer whatever we possess
To the three jewels and to virtuous companions,
To persevere to the extent of our ability
At virtuous karma and at yoga,
To truly engage ourselves in helping those who live
And have become our concern,
To explain the meaning of what we have heard
Through the accumulation of our studies

To those who are fit to receive it:
These four are Dharmas that we are to practice,
Without forgetting the time.

To regret our evils and confess them,
To rejoice at the virtues of others,
To comprehensively dedicate our merits,
And to know that all dharmas are illusory:
These are the four Dharmas of skill in means.

We must study in these ways,
For they are described as the things we must learn
To develop an enlightened attitude that is engaged.

There are no dharmas that do not observe conditions,
And due to this observance they are not made up by their natures,
Or by any specific quality, such as their cessation.

Once we understand that all dharmas are free from complications
We immerse ourselves in keeping a balanced mind
In which we have no anticipations,
And so we are liberated from the chains
Of taking things on and holding onto them.

This wisdom is the practice ground for holy ones.
It is a real enlightenment,
And is the ultimate enlightened attitude.

It is only acquired through the Dharma itself,
So in order for our minds to reach the end
We must perfect our virtues
Through generosity, the rule of the way,
Patience, diligence, meditation, and wisdom.

We work to fulfill the objectives of other beings
By distributing goods and services, speaking pleasantly,
Meaningful practices, and accommodating objectives,
And we respectfully demonstrate peaceful abiding and higher seeing
As we travel over the paths of accumulation and application,

Till we embark upon the path of seeing,
Where we comprehend all the levels:
Brilliant Joy, the Stainless, Light Maker,

Advice to Kublai Khan

Diffusion of Light, Difficult Study, Making it Real,
Gone So Far, Unperturbed, The Intelligence of the Good,
And Cloud of Dharma,
And we progressively actualize their virtues
Till we have entirely completed the path of meditation.

Then, on the path that goes to the end,
We eliminate obstructions and habituations,
Till we do not move from the embodiment of the Dharma,
Which is the single taste of our dominion and our wisdom.
Our bodies blaze with the marks and exemplary features,
Being inseparable from the five wisdoms.

We teach the Dharma of the Supreme Vehicle
With melodious voices that have sixty cadences,
And we completely enjoy the inexhaustible bliss
Of being at one with our children.

This is unchanging and its river is not dammed,
So in an effort to accommodate the wishes of living beings
We totally illuminate the variety of all things
For everyone,
Till we discover the station of fulfilling the intentions of everyone,
And we make these manifest.

Then we use the wheel of inexhaustible adornments,
For so long as samsara's wheels may turn,
As an adornment for this world and its peace,
And we use the traditional ways,
In keeping with our innumerable excellent lifetimes from of yore,
To achieve Buddhahood.

The children of the Victorious One
Who live in the present
Will not be held back for long
In becoming things like these.

Those who engage themselves in these things
Will, in the future, be Buddhas.
This is why I beg you to use this way
For the glory of the world and its peace.

Chogyal Phagpa

Your ancestral line will take its proper birth
Among the holy,
For this is the brilliance of the highest glory and endowment.

Should Prince Nomo Khan order it in full from afar,
I will elucidate the ways of two classic traditions.

This glorification of our teacher
Follows on the trails of transmission and scripture,
And it is explained that we are to use reason when we inquire of them.

When your heart is summoned by faith,
Listen to these virtuous compositions from my mind.
I beg you to listen to it with someone else reading it,
Or else to take a look at it.

I have not studied very much
Of the wisdom that is in the mandalas
Of scripture and what must be known.
So I beg the holy ones
That come to receive this,
Wherever they may be,
To think upon it tolerantly.

By any virtue that may born from this,
May I and all who live
Embark on the path of the supreme vehicle,
And attain the status of Buddhahood.

This Glorification, a letter to prince Nomo Khan, was composed in full by Phagpa, one who took the dust off the feet of the Dharma Lord Sakya Pandita, who was most wise and had no fears about any Dharma, to the crown of his head, in the male water monkey year (1272/73 A.D.) during the eleventh month, which is when the Tathagata demonstrated many miracles, on the eleventh day.

The secretary was named Atsara.

Advice to Kublai Khan

A ROSARY OF BENEFICENCE: A DISCOURSE FOR PRINCE MANGGALA

rGyal bu manga la la gtam du bya ba

I bow to all the Buddhas and Bodhisattvas.

The glorious Buddha has a glorious body,
Attractive and beneficent.
His speech engages in all things,
Unstoppable and beneficent.
His heart is playful
In the knowledge and love of beneficence.
He has a full store of beneficence.
I bow to him.

The young prince is endowed with the signs of beneficence,
And has commissioned me to do this,
So I am making a critical examination
Of the Victorious One's scriptures,
Their transmission and their reasoning,
Stylistically developing on their beneficence,
And offering it to you.

This is how it is:
The high status that you have attained,
With its full store of glory and good things,
Did not come about because you took hold of it
Under your own initiative.

Even your body is something that someone else gave birth to,
And for this reason you were born.
This was not done by some well-known creator:
The sky, or a god, or by luck.
Eternity and a creator are contradictory.

On the whole, the objectives of this world
Are perceived in keeping with what we are looking for.
So it is that our happiness and sorrow in this world
Are, on the whole, brought forth due to our karma.
This is what the Sage has said.
It can also be proven by reason.
This is why we must be respectful
With regard to virtuous karma,
For this is what makes us happy.

The conditions that operate synchronously with it:
Your acceptance into the lineage of your father and mother,
As well as the trifling assistances you have received from others,
Are discrete kindnesses for which favors must be returned.

When you do this,
The virtues from your past will be truly augmented,
Others who come after you will follow up on them,
And through your escalation of virtue for everyone,
Both yourself and other beings,
There will occur a beneficence
That reaches to the frontiers of your constituency.
Count on it.

The Sage has given us brilliant proclamations
Regarding the seven attributes of high status.
They are our families, bodies, wisdom, and pleasures,
Our dominion, our lack of illness, and our long lives.
These are things to be safeguarded.

It is said that you have been truly born into a prominent family,
This is true,
But you must employ yourself in virtuous projects and practices
To be pure.
Without these practices,
The intentions of your family will have failed.

Advice to Kublai Khan

These things are evidenced so well
In the literary classics.
With regard to virtuous practices for this world
They say that we must duly safeguard
Our not drinking beer,
Clean living,
Not being destructive,
Making offerings to those who deserve them,
And being generous toward the impoverished.

The noble Nagarjuna said,
With his own mouth,
That we should also have shame,
And make use of our embarrassments
To properly restrain ourselves,
To turn away from deeds that are ridiculed by everyone,
And brilliantly persevere in deeds that are praiseworthy,
As well as to discontinue the things we have done of yore,
And do things that will excite our body-hairs,
Things that harm no one,
And that help everyone:
To build parks around libraries and reliquaries,
To provide housing for the indigent,
So as to wave the banner of our renown
In the ten directions.

These are, exclusively, the kinds of things that are good.
You must employ yourself in things like this
To make your maternal heritage shine.

You must get personally involved in them.
These sorts of projects
Are totally spacious and are astounding.

So make use of the assembled multitudes
To strive towards building palaces,
Adjoining buildings, bathing houses,
Pastures for horses, garden yards, and fountains.

In the current situation,
These things will be delightful and amazing.
You will have done an outstanding service to yourself.

You will make use of the virtues you have gathered from of yore.
And you will once again make flourish
The things that you yearn for.

For these reasons,
You must maintain the utmost dignity
With regard to the ways of such things.

To succeed at whatever may please you,
Be without unmentionables,
And use the things that others have presented you
In an appropriate manner.
This is the foundation for the endowment of high status,
And is like a boat,
For it is the basis or structure
By which we make it to the other side
Of the ocean of this world.

It makes our senses clear,
Augments our physical strength,
And assures that we stay in contact with happiness
For a long time.
So it is that we must safeguard it
As if it were a lotus on the water,
By providing the requisites that maintain life,
Such as food and medicine,
With due respect for the country, the time,
And the current situation.

We should bathe to wash away our filth,
Till a radiant complexion emerges,
Then put on new clothes that are not overly glamorous,
Then use fresh flowers with a fine aroma,
To make things beautiful,
So that we too may engage in the glories of the gods.
This is evidenced in our traditions.

Wisdom makes both ourselves and others shine.
It is a lamp.
It is the hero who overcomes the pomposity
Of those who quarrel.
It totally rouses that fame that is but a pleasantry.

Advice to Kublai Khan

For these reasons,
You must augment your wisdom.

The wisdom we acquire as a birthright
Will be in keeping with our karma from of yore.
The wisdom we acquire through study
Will depend on our own pursuit.
So I beg you to strive
To make the clarity of your brilliant knowledge shine.

The wonders of our bodies may reach
The thresholds that we can measure,
And the wonders of training toward virtuosity
Are indeed superior to the rest,
And are what everyone else will praise.
You can actually see this.

Wisdom, however, has no form,
And for this reason, it has no threshold.
Its wondrousness has no limitations.
Hence it is an enabler.
This is why we must endow ourselves
With the glory of its unlimited wondrousness.

It is said that if we joyfully memorize one word
From an edition of the teachings that is needful to us,
Every day,
It will not take long till we become wise.
This is how it is with the castles of the ants,
And with honey.
This is found in the proclamations of the Mahatmas.
When we use this method
To acquire, audit, and properly evaluate them,
Using detailed analytics,
The brilliance of our knowledge will grow
Like the waxing of the moon.

The things we have
Augment our joy and happiness,
And those of others,
Both consummate and temporary,
And when we use them methodically,
The pleasure we get from propagating

Chogyal Phagpa

The glories of both this world and its peace
Will never be exhausted.

Then there are the things that resemble
The honey made by bees.
They are rigorously accumulated
Through great personal exertion,
But are not made use of,
And are stolen away by other beings.
Such possessions are the pursuits
Of the poorest of the poor.

The fierce wild animals watch the deer.
They have no love for them,
But steal them away to other places
Where they devour them,
And use them as gifts.
This is the propagation of sorrow.
It resembles food laced with poison.

We may augment our treasuries,
And the survey of our lands,
With things we have not worked for,
And that others have left to be taken,
But when we neither use them,
Nor make gifts of them,
These possessions are like jewels out in the ocean.

Regardless of what we acquire,
When we start out by looking at what there is,
And make use of it for our own happiness in the interim,
And then disperse it among others in the proper way,
These possessions resemble the glory of the gods.

The things that we acquire spontaneously
Are not to be used for works
That are merely on our own behalf.
When we enjoy them by making offerings
To those that are worthy of offerings,
And to properly care for the lowly,
They will be an inexhaustible and magnificent treasure.

Advice to Kublai Khan

So distribute the seeds of kindness
That are in harmony with the nation
To bring peace to your government and its subjects,
So that they may engage in enterprises
That are in conformity with the proper way,
And then the holy ones who are committed to the laws
Will look after them.

Then any of the wealth and glory that they generate,
Such as the milk from horses,
Or the incense from sāla trees,
May, when the time is right,
Be duly taxed,
And this may be collected without doing harm
To augment your holy treasuries.

Then you yourself may enjoy an abundance of delights,
In keeping with the way,
Make offerings to others,
And duly grant them prosperity.
This will make your joy and happiness flourish,
Both now and in the future.

It will cause the prosperity
Of business people, ranchers, and those who work for wages
To flourish,
For this is the way of the common people.
Through such measures their livelihoods
Will be gracefully extended,
So I beg you to grant them livelihoods,
Without doing them harm.

There are commodities that sentient beings use in common,
Such as salt.
We do work to acquire these requisites.
All of them are made possible
Through the private enterprise of the populace.
What do you think about letting them employ themselves like this?

There are things like beer, water, and pens,
That we produce through private enterprise,
And when we sell them,
They contribute to our livelihoods.

We call this: "Making a living through yogurt and meat."
I estimate that it is proper that these things be allowed,
As is described in the scriptures.

There are a few things that we didn't have in the past,
Merchandise that we actually use,
Such as clothing and jewelry.
People always compliment them,
They say: "The gods have them for their entire lives."
Please endorse their development.

It is the prayer of the students of virtue, the Brahmins, and others,
Those who possess both understanding and repute,
That you use your awareness to encourage these things,
For many who yet live delight in them,
And you do no harm when you promote them,
For they are, in fact, the virtues of this world.

Flocks of geese gather
On lakes covered with lotuses in full bloom,
Even thought they might be driven away.
I beg you to allow the populace to gather,
As do the geese,
For they do no harm to your nation's dominion,
And they maintain its wealth.

A consummately mighty lord
Cannot be obstructed by anyone else,
And is capable of protecting
A multitude of living beings.
This is how mighty lords prosper.

Yet they are the same as poisonous snakes
When they dictate things like
Massacre, whipping, torture, and plunder,
Imprisoning rulers and confiscating possessions.
These things are unspeakable,
And must be relinquished.

One who employs honest ways for themselves
Will use honest and reasonable ways
To organize others.
He will eliminate unreasonable practices

Advice to Kublai Khan

By his very character.
One who embarks on the path of reason
Is a mighty lord who is holy.

To be free of illness
Is a supreme happiness.
To make it so that you, personally, are without disease,
You must totally expunge
That portion of things that make illness flourish
In your foods, drinks, homes, and general behaviors,
And that ravish your physical condition,
So that diseases will not be generated
And so that they will be pacified.

You must demonstrate the way we use our homes and requisites
To make our health and senses shine.
Do this with friendship and deferential treatment
In helping those who are sick.
Provide things like medicine, food, clothes, and carpets,
Which are requisites for staying alive,
And help them by making use of a variety of sciences,
Such as mantras.

You must persevere in voicing your recitations,
And such yogas as the Medicine Guru,
The Lord of the World,
And the Goddess of the Mountains who is Covered in Leaves,
And beg them to be active in our nation's many constituencies.

Those who have the attitudes of elemental spirits,
Who use their powers to develop a multiplicity of diseases,
Such as the carnivorous dakinis,
Must be pacified.
To do this, you must issue a command
That offerings be given them,
And services performed for them.

These things will bring happiness to your person,
And through the power of friendship,
All those who live downstream from you,
Who happen to be the subjects of your government,
Will live in happiness,
They will have no disease and they will do no harm.

On the whole, you will be successful,
But to live in contact with happiness for a long time,
And to quest for the Dharma's objectives.
The occasion will come
When you must extend your life-span.

Medicine, samadhi, and secret mantras
Are the things by which we eradicate obstructions,
And have been proclaimed to augment our life-spans,
So I beg you to work diligently
Toward success with these things.

The things that will supplement
The glory and endowments of your life
Are ransoming the lives of those who will surely die,
Granting fearlessness to the lives of those who yet live,
And discontinuing the murder of other beings.

So I beg you to persevere
With Amitayus, Vijaya, and other yogas,
And to continue your recitations,
Adding to them a multitude of services
That you perform to truly sponsor them.
This will totally extend the length of your life.

The seven glories of the high status you have acquired
Are due to your virtuous activities and prayers
From of yore,
The methodical ways that I present you
Will make them grow,
And you will truly be high.

So it is that through the glories of this world
We will consummately fill our stores in this world,
And through the glories that are beyond this world
We establish an endowment for ourselves,
And for everyone else.
For this reason I implore you
To support the path of the Dharma.

This Dharma presents three trainings
That we must talk about.

Advice to Kublai Khan

It maintains stainless spoken words
On three active practices.
From start to finish, and for the duration,
It grants fruition to our virtues.
And there is more,
Which you must learn about elsewhere.

Regarding the impermanence of all compounded things,
We have been given the words:
"All things are lacking in a self,
They are corruptible, and sorrowful.
Nirvana is to be peaceful and happy."
These are the four mudras.

Now these things occurred to the Mighty Sage himself
In reference to his personal conditions,
So they are what we call Proclamations.
They are statements the Sage has made,
And we use the force they represent exclusively
To keep our minds free from disturbances.
For they connect us with the path,
On which we will succeed at being free.

Now there are contradictory ideas
In the commentaries[17] on them.
These are transmitted scriptures about the Dharma.
When we meditate on them,
Our intuitions are heightened.
This is the Dharma of Understanding.

These are the pathways
By which we free ourselves from attachments.
To use them to be free from attachments
Is the Dharma of Cessation.

When we analyze these Dharmas,
We come to understand other things:
The people, the words, and their implications.

To rely on the meaning of the words,
The meaning of the Dharma,

---

[17] bsTan bcos

Chogyal Phagpa

The meaning that is sure,
And the reliance on wisdom,
Have been proclaimed to be the Four Reliances.

The first two of these are pure.
The third is used for our analytics,
The forth is what we depend on.

When we engage in these four,
We progressively acquire five Dharmas,
So they are definitely good Dharmas.
Through them we realize eight things in three parts,
Which we then consolidate into two vehicles.

Now the way of the Dharma,
As used by the Small Vehicle,
Will bring us a personal peace.
This is true,
But it will not bring us Buddhahood.

On it, we must persevere in fasting,
And similar practices,
To the extent of our ability.

We do this to be free from eight discomforting abodes:
Births in the hells, among the ghosts,
As an animal or long-lived god,
Among the savage and those who see things perversely,
In places where Victorious Ones are absent,
Or among the brutish.

When our minds are motivated by desire, hatred, or stupidity,
And we then lie, steal, are carnally perverted,
We deceive, quibble, are cruel with our words, or speak hypocritically.
We are avaricious, spiteful, or perverse in our views,
These are the karmas of darkness,
And it has been proclaimed that we must relinquish them.

When we are human, born in a central nation,
With senses intact, and with faith in our nation,
Where we do not revert to extreme karmas,
Where Buddhas have appeared in our fields,
And have proclaimed the Dharma,

Advice to Kublai Khan

Where their teachings remain,
So that there are those who practice after them,
And where we are taken lovingly onto their trails,
These are the ten endowments.

So we must be motivated by non-attachment,
Have no hatred,
And be without stupidity,
So that we are friendly to those who live,
Disperse our possessions, be desireless,
And speak the truth,
We must work in cooperation,
Speak pleasantly and meaningfully,
We must know contentment and desire to help,
And have the correct perspective.
These have been proclaimed to be
The ten pathways of the karma of light.

So I beg you to strive to achieve them
Under every circumstance.
Furthermore, there are the ten practices of the Dharma:
Writing letters, making offerings, listening,
Reading, memorizing, explaining,
Reciting, chanting, contemplating, and meditating.
Please do these things as much as possible.

The Sage has given us these words:
"Go for refuge, even into the gates of the ambrosial Mahayana,"
So in an effort to protect both ourselves and others
From the fears of samsara and from horrible lives,
And so that we might have faith in our objectives,
We do these things:

We request shelter, until such time
That we achieve the status of the foremost of refuges,
From all the Buddhas,
Who abide in the ten directions,
From all the holy Dharmas,
Which include the finest of vehicles,
And from everyone in the noble Sangha.

We do not assume that things that are not these refuges
Will protect us.

We must make friends with holy people,
Hear from them about the holy Dharma,
And totally persevere in working things out
In conformity with the holy Dharma.

We must repeatedly propagate an enlightened attitude,
For it is evident that this is the cause of great compassion,
And it empowers us with a realization of correct understandings.
It is most delightful,
And is the very identity of a magnificent undertaking.

Then we must study the Proclamations,
Just as they are evidenced in the Sutras,
The Heart Essence of the Sky[18] among them,
For as it has been proclaimed:
"We must study and then understand them
So that we may quickly acquire all their goodness and benefits."

You must understand that the reason we are ill
Is the intolerable sorrow of samsara,
And that its source is karma and emotional problems.
Their cessation is a continuing happiness in which we have no disease.
The path resembles a medicine for our lives.

So let this understanding rise in your heart,
Strive to totally relinquish the source of sorrow,
And have a sincere longing for its end,
Then exert yourself at practicing the path.

These have been proclaimed to be the four noble truths.
They are also the vows for the entirety of the Dharma.

Birth, old age, sickness, and death
Are four rivers of sorrow.
They are the conclusions we create
Through piling things up.
The conclusion of loftiness is debasement.
The conclusion of life is death.
The conclusion of getting together is falling apart.
These are proclaimed to be the four conclusions of samsara.

---

[18] Nam mkha'i snying po'i mdo

Advice to Kublai Khan

So I beg you
To fear for yourself and have a heart's love for others,
To ford through yourself and liberate others,
And to free yourself and lead others.

Out of ignorance there is conception.
From it there is consciousness.
From it there is name and form.
Out of them there emerge six generative forces.
Through them there is touch.
From it there are feelings.
Out of these there occurs desire.
From it there is acquisition.
Out of this there is life.
From life there is birth.
From birth there is sickness,
Old age, death, misery, and wailing.
This is unhappiness.

Misery comes to be through the progressions
Of the heaps.
Ignorance is ceased
Through an analysis of material things.
Through this we progressively eliminate conceptions,
And the rest of them.
We free ourselves from sorrow.

These are the twin methods
Regarding dependent origination.

The way things appear to us
Is entirely obscured and relative.
Their true nature is free from complications.
This is their holy significance.
When we examine what this means,
And meditate till we are adept in it,
We will be empowered
Into the Dharmas of the transmission
And its understanding.

Attachments and their kind
Obstruct the path to freedom.
Our understandings of the three contingencies:

An actor, an action, and an object,
Obstruct our omniscience.

I beg you to become holy
In applying the distinct remedies for these obstructions,
And in the wondrous virtues of the path.

Make friends with companions in virtue
Through objectives you agree upon,
Strive to accomplish them,
And endow yourself with four magnificent wheels
To present your holy prayers well.

To acquire things or not acquire them,
To be happy or not be happy,
To be famous or not be famous,
To be praised or to be blamed.
These are the Eight Dharmas.

For those who are level-headed
All of them are a great treasury
In which to immerse ourselves,
For they present the conditions for our virtues.
They are indeed to be worked upon peacefully.

They give us things to work toward success with,
And in the rule of the way
They temporarily bear fruit.

But the refuge of the gods,
And the fruition that goes on till the end,
Is the Buddha, the Dharma, and the Sangha,
So we must recollect the wondrous virtues of each of them.

Faith, giving, the rule of the way,
Study, knowing shame, discretion, and wisdom
Allow us to attain noble status,
And even in the world
They propagate glory and happiness,
So they are called: "The Seven Jewels of Nobility."
This was proclaimed by the most excellent of the nobles.

Advice to Kublai Khan

You must work perpetually
To endow yourself with these finest of jewels.
Others who depend on you
Will then also be so endowed.
Count on it.

Generosity, the rule of the way, patience,
Diligence, dhyāna meditation, and wisdom
Take us to the other side of this world and its peace,
So use these six perfections
To move on toward the other side of this world and its pacification.

Make gifts of goods and services,
Fearlessness, the Dharma, and friendship,
For these are the four kinds of generosity.

Study the rules regarding the vows against non-virtue,
The gathering of Dharmas of virtue,
And acting to help sentient beings.

Pacify your heart with the three kinds of patience:
Not being divisive, having no ulterior motive,
And having an attitude of certitude.

Persevere in the five kinds of diligence:
Armor, engagement in propriety,
Not being dejected, not being upset,
And not being satisfied.

Gather up all the Dharmas of Light
With the two kinds of dhyāna meditation:
Relinquishment and practice toward success,
For they pacify your heart and make your virtues flourish.

Use the intelligence you gain
Through hearing, contemplating, and meditating,
To give birth to that wisdom that understands
Both the relative, which is totally obscured,
And the holy significance,
For they empower you into the entirety of the Dharma,
And make you into a holy potentate
Who will effect a comprehensive transformation.

The four doors to total freedom
Are emptiness, the lack of identifying markings,
Having no aspirations, and not being compounded,
When you understand how it is with them,
You will have reached the perfection of wisdom.
To settle into this with equanimity accordingly
Is dhyāna meditation.

Each of these six is made complete with these four:
Skill in methods, prayer, strength, and wisdom,
So at the end, these four are to be practiced individually.
By them we will reach the end of the ten levels.

I beg you to use these four:
Goods and services, pleasant speaking,
Accommodation of differing objectives,
And targeted practices,
To assemble the multitudes who live,
So that we may work toward magnificent things,
For they are the four real things that bring us together.

Now these three:
The higher rule of the way, samadhi, and wisdom,
Are like our feet and eyes
When we travel the pathways of the noble.
All the Dharmas of Virtue are subsumed in them,
So we must study them with extreme exertion.

Use peaceful abiding,
Which is to keep what we envision and what we do not envision
In balance,
To work on your samadhi.
Use a higher vision to analyze your objectives,
So that you may purify your brilliant knowledge and wisdom.

Use the interaction of merit, which involves complications,
And wisdom, which has no complications,
To make their interaction flourish.
This way you will be endowed with the glory
Of oceans of these two accumulations.

The five kinds of obstruction are called:
Desirous longing, harmful attitudes,

Advice to Kublai Khan

Darkened wildness, regret, and doubt.
They interfere with our acquisition of dhyāna meditation
And happiness.

To keep things in balance,
We must get rid of them bit by bit,
Then we will instill in ourselves a samadhi
That has three kinds of faith in the finest of objectives,
Three kinds of compassion for the lowly,
And three kinds of enlightened attitude.

We will instill in ourselves friendship,
Compassion, joy, and equanimity,
So these will be our stations of purity,
Vast and beyond analogy,
For they are also the Victorious One's Immeasurables.

The four dhyāna meditations
That are associated with the realm of form are:
That which is inclusive of conceptualizations and analysis,
That which takes in joy and delight,
That which is simply happiness,
And the samadhi which is an entirely pure equanimity.

Likewise, the four generative forces[19] associated with the formless are:
The bounteous sky,
Bounteous consciousness,
Nothing at all,
And that which is neither existent nor non-existent.

The eight emancipations[20] are called:
Cessation, the nine kinds of keeping a balance,
That with form, the formless, that which looks at forms,
That which truly makes things beautiful,
The sky, and its consciousness.

The ten exhaustions are called:
The samadhi that exhausts internal and external objects,
And the meditations on the consciousnesses
That regard earth, water, fire, and wind,

---

[19] sKye mched
[20] rNam thar brgyad po

Blue, yellow, red, white, and the sky.

The eight generative forces[21] are:
A consolidated understanding of forms,
In which external forms are subtle, gross, or formless,
Which is a consolidated understanding of forms both great and small.
It, in turn, observes and overwhelms the blue, yellow, red, and white.

When we instill in ourselves these yogas here classified,
We brilliantly blaze through our individual problems,
Which are to be got rid of,
Along with their brambles,
So that we then achieve a holy vision of samadhi.

Our bodies, feelings, dharmas, and minds,
Are impure, sorrowful, selfless, and impermanent.
Once we understand that they have no true nature,
We must remember this.
We use these four to traverse
The smaller path of accumulation.

The development of virtue and its protection,
The non-development of non-virtue,
And renunciation
Are correct relinquishments,
And are associated with diligence.
Please use these four
To reach the end of the middling path of accumulation.

You must use your longings,
Scrutiny, recollection, mind,
Samadhi, understanding, and four magical feet,
To travel to the shores of the greater path of accumulation.

These five:
Faith, diligence, recollection,
Samadhi, and wisdom
Are our five senses.
Through them we are granted empowerment
Into all the Dharmas of virtue.
This takes us to the final summit.

---

[21] sKye mched brGyad

Advice to Kublai Khan

They become powers for us,
And are the five powers.
They overcome every unacceptable position
Regarding the path.
Please use patience along with these excellent Dharmas
To make a journey on the path of application.

Recollection, discrimination of the Dharmas, diligence,
Delight, comprehensive study, samadhi, and equanimity:
Use these seven branches of enlightenment
For the path of seeing.
After you have seen everything,
You must find liberation.

When your life is in danger,
You are dying,
Or are frightened
Because you are surrounded in a horrible and infamous life,
Give up these five abodes of trepidation,
For you will have become the only concern for the supremely noble.

Correct view, livelihood, seeking, recollection,
Samadhi, speech, ends of karma, and thought:
These are the eight paths of the noble.
They take us to the ends of the path of meditation.
Now the paths are also subdivided into ten levels:
Brilliant Joy, the Stainless, Light Maker, Diffusion of Light,
Difficult Cleansing, Making it Real, Gone so Far, the Unshaking,
Good Intellect and Cloud of Dharma.
When we are on Brilliant Joy
We acquire a hundred samadhis,
All at one time,
We engage in them.
We see a hundred Buddhas,
And know their blessings.
We go to a hundred pure lands,
And all the realms of the world tremble.
We illuminate these hundred,
And bring a hundred beings to maturity.
We remain for a hundred eons,
And are engaged to the ends of the past and the future.
We open a hundred Dharmas,
And reveal a hundred bodies.

Each of these bodies is surrounded by a retinue
Of a hundred Bodhisattvas.
So its wondrous virtues are twelve hundreds.

Those who reside on the Stainless,
On up to those on the tenth level
Respectively have a thousand,
A hundred thousand,
A hundred ten millions,
A thousand ten millions,
A hundred thousand ten millions,
Ten million hundred thousand millions,
A number equal to the atoms in a hundred thousand worlds,
Or likewise the atoms in innumerable hundreds of thousands of worlds,
Or a number equal to the atoms in worlds without end.

In the end,
We use the vajra-like Samadhi
To totally expunge the grime
That would bring us to bad places.

We will have reached the end
Of the paths there are to follow.
This is called the path that makes it to the end.
This is when we get rid of our obstructions,
And the inclinations that go with them,
And where our dominion and our wisdom
Have one taste.

This is a consummate purging.
It is also our natural embodiment in the Dharma.
We do not shift away from this inexhaustible domain,
So our two accumulations are fully completed,
And our prayers will have come true.

This is, in fact, the natural embodiment of the Dharma.
We do not shift away from this inexhaustible domain,
While our two embodiments are entirely perfected
And our prayers are all well fulfilled.

We do not dwell on the frontiers of this world
Or of its peace,
But focus on the appearance of pure wisdom.

Advice to Kublai Khan

In the indestructible pure land that is called Akaniṣṭa
We dwell in the cloud of the Dharma,
In an oceanic assembly
Where only the supreme vehicle is proclaimed,
And for a duration of time that has no future ending
We remain in concourse with the mandala that is our entourage
In an embodiment that enjoys inexhaustible joy and happiness.
This is the Body of Perfect Enjoyment.

Our bodies transform their stations
Into an unchanging vajra.
Our feet and hands are marked by wheels.
We have the feet of tortoises.
Our fingers and toes are connected by webs.
Our hands and feet are smooth,
And their flesh is youthful.

The forefront of a Sage's body is lofty.
The fingers are long.
The rear is expansive.
The body is erect.
The arches of the feet are not evident.
The body hair stands out straight.
The calves are like an Enaya.
The arms are long and beautiful.
The privates that are his genitals are drawn inward
In an excellent discretion.
His skin has a golden hue,
And this skin is tight.
Each of his body hairs comes out clockwise.
His eyebrows are adorned with connecting hairs.
His upper body resembles a lion's.
His elbows are rounded.
The palms are wide.
He perceives things with the most excellent taste,
Even though things might not taste delicious.
His body is symmetrical,
Like a nyagrodha bodhi tree.
He has a knotted crown of hair protruding.
His tongue is handsomely long.
He has the voice of Brahma.
His cheeks are like a lion's.
His teeth are extremely white.

They are even and have a fine texture.
Their full number is forty.
His eyes are dark blue,
And his eyelashes are fine.
These are the thirty-two markings.
Such are the very finest of markings.

His nails are the hue of copper,
Glossy and rounded at the top.
His fingers are quite wide, exuding refinement.
The veins are not obvious,
And there are no knotted veins.
His ankle bones are not obvious,
And the soles of his feet are entirely even.
He moves forward starting with his right,
After the manner of lions, elephants, the kings of geese, and buffalo.
He moves beautifully,
His body tending to move around or circumvent things,
As if he were sweeping up.
He is aligned with the progressions of total beauty.
He is fully complete in the signs of cleanliness, gentleness, and purity.
His body's limbs are wide and most excellent.
His steps are even.
His eyes are clear.
His skin retains its youth.
He is not timid, but expansive.
His body is well poised.
His limbs are distinct.
His vision is without astigmatism.
His buttocks is round,
And his body does not stagger when he moves.
His belly is firm,
And his navel is deep.
It twists clockwise,
And is entirely beautiful.
He is cleanly in everything he does.
His body has no moles.
His hands are so very smooth,
Like the wool from trees.
The outline of his hand shines and glows;
It is deep and long.
His face is not overly long.
It is proportionate.

Advice to Kublai Khan

His complexion is reddish like a *bimpa* fruit.
His tongue is smooth and soft.
It is reddish like the hue of copper.
His voice is that of a dragon,
And his speech is soft.
His canine teeth are rounded and sharp.
They are even and brilliantly white.
His calves are fine.
His nostrils and upper nose are clean.
His eyes are wide.
His eyelashes are quite thick,
With the white separate from the black.
His eyebrows are long, smooth, and glossy.
His body hairs are even.
His hands are wide.
His ears are even.
They do not droop down.
His forehead has lines.
Its breadth is large.
His head is large.
His hair is the color of a bee.
It is thick, smooth, and neither shaggy nor ragged.
It is sweet smelling.
His hands and feet are marked with the seal of the glory of well-being.
These are the eighty exemplary markings.
The excellent body of our protector
Is beautified by such as these.

Our speech is transformed in station
To become a speech that does not stop.
It is ornamented by sixty cadences of melody.
It is pleasant, smooth, attractive, and accommodating to the mind.
It is pure, stainless, clear, harmonious,
Worth hearing, not intimidating, agreeable, and subdued.
It is neither cruel nor rude.
It is well controlled and flowing.
It satisfies our bodies and it satisfies our minds.
It is delightful to our minds.
It is joyous, happy, and pleasant.
It removes torment and makes us omniscient.
It makes us understand and is clear in detail.
Listening to it brings joy and true delight.
It makes us fully comprehend omniscience.

It is reasonable and without faulty utterance.
It is melodious like the voices of lions, elephants, and dragons,
And it is pleasant like the voices of the mighty nagas,
Of gandharvas, kalapingga birds,
And the melodies of Brahma, cranes, and sparrows.
It is brilliant like the melodies of the mighty gods
And the voices of drums.
It is neither arrogant nor demeaning,
While it accommodates every language.
The words are not broken into pieces,
And there is no lack of completeness.
It is neither dejected nor avaricious.
It is brilliantly joyous.
It is comprehensive and firm in intention.
It fills in breaks in the flow and the connections between words.
It satisfies our senses without denigration or altercation.
It is not confrontational,
And it resounds through every near-by circle.
It is endowed with excellence in its every aspect.
It is profound.
It demonstrates the way of the great vastness of the Dharma.

Our minds transform in station
Into a heart of non-duality,
Which may be divided into the twin wisdoms
That comprehend the way things are and the ways they are enumerated,
And the works that they support.

We have the five wisdoms that are called:
The dominion of the Dharma,
That which is like a mirror,
That of equality,
That of the comprehension of particulars,
And that which gets things done.

Our faults transform in station
To become inexhaustible virtues.
There are the thirty-seven Dharmas directed toward enlightenment.
There are the four immeasurables.
There are the eight emancipations.

Likewise, there are the nine aspects of keeping things in balance
That of form, the formless, and the observance of forms,

Advice to Kublai Khan

The sky which actually makes things beautiful,
The consciousness,
There being nothing at all,
The absence of existence,
The absence of non-existence,
And cessation.

Then there are the ten exhaustions,
Which are known to be meditations on our consciousness:
Earth, water, fire, air, blue, yellow, red, white, sky, and space.
These employ our consciousness of forms,
Both subtle and gross,
And their formation.
We observe both small and large forms,
As well as blue, yellow, red, and white,
And we overwhelm them,
So these are the eight overwhelmings.

We will personally have no emotional problems,
So we will overcome the emotional problems of others,
Till there will be no emotional problems.
Through our prayers we will spontaneously understand
All the Dharmas that are to be known,
And we will cut through all doubt.

We will have knowledge, miracles,
And divine eyes and ears.
We will know the minds of our opponents,
Know our previous stations,
And comprehend the exhaustion of our emissions.
These are called: "The six supernatural cognitions."

These are the Dharmas that are to be explained.
Their meanings and the act of explaining them are called:
"Words of certainty and of audacity."

There are four kinds of distinctly correct understanding.
The four entire purities are:
Our support, our objective, our heart, and our wisdom.

Likewise there are the ten powers,
Which have been proclaimed to be life, mind, provisions, works,
Reverence, rebirth, prayer, miracle, wisdom,

And strength in the Dharma.

There are also the ten strengths:
Our abode, our works, the conditions we aspire to,
The paths our senses travel,
The cleansing of our emotional problems,
Laughter, memory of our previous dwellings,
Death, transfer, rebirth,
And the knowledge that our emissions have been exhausted.

In the discovery of wisdom,
The relinquishment of what must be abandoned,
The path of decisive revulsion,
And the teaching of how to discontinue,
We have no timidity at all.
These are called: "The four kinds of fearlessness."

To be completely pure in our physical, verbal, and mental engagements,
To have nothing to hide,
And to guard nothing:
These are three.

A heart that does not become emotional about these three:
What we long for,
What we do not long for,
And what is in-between.
These are the three true stations of recollection.

To have no complacency regarding the purposes of others,
To be rid of obstructions that are associated with our habits,
To have a great compassion that considers the welfare of all,
Not to settle ourselves in delusion or cacophony,
To have no failings in our memory,
Or prejudicial conceptions,
Or equanimities that are not judicious:
These are the six consolidations of our practice.

Not to fail in our aspirations,
Our exertion,
Our memory,
Our samadhi,
Our knowledge,
Or the total freedom of our wisdom:

Advice to Kublai Khan

These are the six consolidations of our understanding.

The three consolidations
By which our wisdom is without impediment
Throughout the three times,
And by which we keep to the tracks of wisdom
In the deeds of our body, speech, and mind
Are the consolidations of our good work.
These are the eighteen unadulterated Dharmas.

The Tathagata has all these.
He is omniscient with regard to the basis and the path that goes with it.
These are, in turn, the twenty-one subdivisions of inexhaustibility,
And they are entirely consolidated in his wondrous virtues.
They are also counted to be
The embodiment of the Dharma that we understand.

Our karma is transformed in station,
To become the Victorious One's good works.
We organize our disciples
In the glory of true highness.
We lead them along the paths of the three vehicles,
And, till we reach the end,
We work toward their attainment of Buddhahood.
These are the five kinds of good works.
Proclamations on the twenty-seven kinds of good works
Are summarized within these.
You must know this.

Such things as these
Are the fruition of what we propagate on the path.
We use them according to the differences
In our conditions and in those we are to train,
For these are the movements in our domain,
And each one,
According to their individual fortune,
Will manifest differentially,
For so long as the bounteous father lives in the world.
We work toward their individual objectives.
This is the manifest embodiment of the Buddha.

The five things that it manifests are
To be born, and to build,

Great enlightenment, nirvana,
And a variety of teachings.
This is the consummate store of our understanding.

And so it is that the highest sage
Moves his mind through the dominion of the Dharma,
As it is but of one flavor,
And has no beginning,
For due to the bounteousness of these conditions,
Under which both merit and wisdom have been stored,
He is truly born.
He overcomes dis-accommodating positions,
Right at the root,
And discovers the endowment of empowerment
That is within every Dharma.

He makes all holy dreams come true,
And there is an undammed river of objectives
For his works.
For these reasons he is eternal and stable,
For his river is not to be dammed,
And the Dharmas that he teaches do not fail.

The Sangha that studies them rises up systematically,
And therefore will not be obstructed.

So I beg you to take them as refuges,
And to act like them.

This is a request that you will fulfill.
There is nothing else for you to do
Than to be outstanding in this work.
Doing this, you will have done everything.
It's worth doing.
It's the best thing you can do.
It takes you to the end.

I was verbally commanded.
By Prince Manggala,
To present this,
So in an effort to help the one who commissioned it,
And other people,
I, the monk Phagpa, composed it.

Advice to Kublai Khan

This is surely so,
But I have not done a vast study of the transmitted Dharma,
And I don't have any understanding.
I beg the patience of the one who commissioned this,
And the holy ones who come to receive it.
By its virtues may I and every sentient being
Quickly attain Buddhahood.

For the present,
May the ones who commissioned this,
Husband, wife, and children,
Have no illness, live long lives, and be virtuous.

This is a brilliant work that will grant the fruition
Of miraculous beneficence.
I was repeatedly encouraged to write it
By Tashi Gyaltsan.
The secretary was named Atsara.

This brilliant work demonstrates both true highness and ascertained goodness. It is called: A Discourse for Prince Manggala: A Rosary of Beneficence. I, Phagpa, a monk who took the dust from the feet of the Dharma Lord Sakya Pandita to the crown of my head, composed it during the male fire rat year (1276-77 A.D.), on the first day of the month of *sPo*, when the star of victory had come out. It was completed in the area of Dokham.

Chogyal Phagpa

LIGHT RAYS FROM THE MOON: CONFIDENTIAL ADVICE FOR PRINCE DEMUR BHOGA

rGyal bu de mur bho ga la nye bar gdams pa zla ba'i 'od zer

I bow to all the Buddhas and Bodhisattvas.

There is one whose excellent body was born out of patience,
With the sweet smell of the rule of the way,
Brilliantly endowed with the glory of generosity,
Who achieved his purpose through diligence,
Who found peace through dhyāna meditations,
Who used the perfections to go on to the other side,
The total freedom of the highest wisdom.
I bow to him.

Having been so ordered
By the command of the prince,
The Grand Arog,
I, Phagpa, am sending this letter of confidential advice
To his son, Demur Bhoga.

The holy Dharma is the only thing
That brings welfare and happiness
To both ourselves and others,
In the present and through all our lifetimes.

So put all your other engagements into equanimity,
And exert yourself in the engagements of the holy Dharma.

I pray that you persevere in this in everything you do.

This Dharma has come into existence
Through the personal initiative
Of the perfect Buddha.
Its unstained words of oration
Teach three kinds of trainings:
The rule of the way, samadhi, and wisdom.
It is ascertained through three validations.
It is virtuous from the beginning right up to the end.
This is why it is called: "The holy Dharma."

It includes the Discipline, the Sutras, and the Abhidharma.
These are called: "The three baskets."
They are divided up according to the significance orated on.
They include summarized teachings, melodious proclamations,
Prophesies, verses, intentional statements, basic topics,
And a section that talks about ideas.
There are also the histories,
The presentations on the succession of lives.
The occurrence of miracles, and the extremely vast.
These are called: "The twelve branches of the orations."
They include all the vehicles of the Auditors.
They also include the supreme vehicle,
For while their ways are similar,
It is especially noble.

We write commentaries on these ways,
Both general and on particular topics.
These are called: "Commentaries."

All of these are called: "The Dharma of Scripture."
A summary of their practices
Is that we are frightened by the horrors of samsara,
And the fear of horrible existences,
So we must protect others in every way.

To do this, right up to the point we achieve
The level of fearlessness,
With devotion, we forever go for refuge
To the Buddha, the Dharma, and the Sangha,
As our teacher, the path, and our friends,
For they are the thing we must attain,

Advice to Kublai Khan

The thing that must be taught,
And the entourage.

This is the doorway at which we embark onto the Dharma.
This is also the foundation of the path.

When we are stable in these refuges,
We will know the wonders of the Jewels,
And we will constantly remember them.

When we are in pain,
We solicit them,
So that we ourselves and other beings
May be free.

When we are happy,
We remember that they are our refuge,
And that this is due to their kindness.

They shelter us from every fear.
They are a stable foundation of wondrous virtues.
The shelter they provide is the best.

At first, we think only of those who are like us,
Those who relied on the Buddhas of yore
In their work for the welfare of all sentient beings,
And to attain Buddhahood.
They developed the finest of attitudes,
Persevered on the finest of paths,
And found enlightenment.
We say: "I too will be like them."

Then, in the visible presence of our guru,
The Buddhas of the ten directions,
As well as their children,
We give birth to the finest enlightened attitude,
One that is identified with both prayer and applications.

We recollect the problems that there are
With both samsara and nirvana,
And we do not wish to be part of them.
We recollect all the wondrous virtues
There are in the highest enlightenment,

And we yearn for them.

Sentient beings equal to the sky,
With none excepted,
Have been our fathers, mothers,
Or some sort of friend,
And they are like we are.
When we truly understand this,
We will love them,
And our minds will become empowered.

So we say: "I will work toward the highest enlightenment
So that I may get them to the highest happiness."
When our prayer for enlightenment is stable,
We act on the intention that it expresses.
We turn away from evil.
If something evil should happen,
We confess it,
And we strive to the extreme toward virtue.

We also dedicate things to enlightenment,
And apply everything toward helping others.
We use the interactivity of emptiness and compassion
To thoroughly train our minds in every way.
This is the application of enlightenment.

We use generous contributions of anything we may possess
To traverse the path.
We guard the rule of the way to the extent of our ability.
We use patience
To give birth to the glory of peace.
We use diligence
To consolidate the Dharmas of the light.
We use the peace of samadhi
To cleanse our minds.
We brilliantly propagate wisdom
To become holy lords of the Dharma.

What is more,
When we distribute goods and services,
We bring living beings together,
And expound on the Dharma.
Once we are delighted with its agreeable objectives,

Advice to Kublai Khan

We apply ourselves to practicing what they mean.

So it is that through expertise in the methods of gathering,
In peaceful abiding and higher insight,
We gather up our stores on the path of accumulation.
Then we use the path of applications toward total freedom.

Once we are thoroughly engaged,
We use the path of seeing
To see the universal pathway
Of the dominion of the Dharma.

We become accustomed to meditation,
And use entirely pure yogas
To traverse the ten levels.

Then we use the path that goes to the end,
And when we have reached the end
Of the traversing that we had to do,
Our dominion and our wisdom
Will be of one taste,
In the full store of our position and understanding.

We spontaneously take on an embodiment and wisdom,
And in holy enlightenment,
We become Buddhas.

I beg you to do this personally.

So I have explained a little, in clear words,
The significance of the oceanic way of the Dharma,
For Demur Bhoga.
I recommend that you look at it during the daytime.

Through any virtue that may be born from this
May everyone alive,
The one who addresses you
And the nation with the instructions being foremost,
Attain the status of Buddhahood.

Light Rays from the Moon: Advice for Prince Demur Bhoga was written in the year of the male fire rat (1276/77 A.D.) on the twenty-third day of the month of the Horse Star. The secretary who brought it up to the sky was Atsara.

A FOUNTAIN OF AMBROSIA: CONFIDENTIAL ADVICE FOR PRINCE DEGUS BHOGA

rGyal bu de gus bho ga la nye bar gdams pa bdud rtsi'i 'byung gnas

I bow to all the Buddhas and Bodhisattvas.

O Prince,
This place where prosperity and happiness spring forth
Is the finest of river banks,
Where we may wash away our problems.
I will bow to the Buddha,
Then present this to you.

When you hear it you will have pleasant words to say.
When you have savored a little,
Your joy and happiness will grow.   ,
When you keep it as a river,
You will propagate the glories of this world and its peace.
This advice is a fountain of ambrosia.

Your father, mother, grandparents, uncles and other relatives
Have embarked through the doors of this ambrosia of immortality,
So they must practice the way of the Dharma,
As is appropriate.
You personally met with the Dharma
Immediately upon being born.
This is through the power of your good prayers.

You have been cared for by virtuous friends.
You have rightly avowed yourself with good vows,
And have been born into the family of the Buddhas.

You must do work that is fitting for this family.
Turn away from evil in what you do.
Persevere at virtue, as is proper.
Use your mind to tame your mind.
Do things that are in keeping with the Sage's orations.
Make a true practice of cleansing your three doors
Of motivations that are emotionally problematic.

The Sage has proclaimed that when we harm others
We get a fruition of sorrow.

When we take lives,
Our lives are short.
We have many ills.
The full fruition
Is that we go to hell.
This is found in the scriptures.

The hot hells have a floor of molten iron.
The Lord of the Dead,
Who is our karma,
Flays us,
And we are cooked in a large copper cauldron,
With its boiling waters of wrath.

Some will get out,
Only to be pierced, pounded, and tormented
By brilliantly blazing weapons.
We will not die
Until our bad karma is exhausted.
This is called: "The transmission of eternal sorrow."
Some will be there for many countings of the years,
Or reside there for an eon.

The cold hells are entirely untouched
By the light of the sun.
We are born amongst snowy mountains,
Where mounds of ice pile up,

Advice to Kublai Khan

Tortured by the wind and the cold.
Numerous bubbles emerge.
They crack open and split into multitudes.
Our blood and pus pour out,
And freeze.
We can't even shiver.
This sorrow will go on
For many enumerations of the years,
Until a so-called: "Death" occurs.

Consider these things,
And in your current situation,
To be an example that applies to your body and your life.
You must turn away from taking lives.

Through taking what is not given
Our pleasures are stolen.
Through the practice of perverted desires
We meet with enemies,
For we are connected to each other through our desires.

For the majority,
The fruition of these kinds of things
Has been proclaimed
To be our entrapment in the life of a hungry spirit.
We are born on islands and under the earth,
In ranges of sand and on sandy desert steppes,
Or in ravines.

We do not even talk about food or drink.
We look for a way to deal with it,
But where do we go?
When we do find a little,
Our karma makes us perceive it to be pus and blood,
But in our hunger we eat it,
As it turns into a fiery ash pit.
We will be tormented by these sorrows
That are difficult to bear
Every day, for the months that count five hundred years.
This is definitely to be found in the scriptures that are correct.

Think about this,
And consider the example for yourself.

You must turn away from taking what is not given
And from perverted desires,
In all their forms.

When we speak in lies,
We are deceived by others.
Through gossip we lose our friends.
When we speak randomly our words are not respected.
Through speaking cruel words
We will be ridiculed by others.
Through covetousness our hopes are dashed.
A harmful attitude brings us a lot of harm.

We will experience the dharmas that are visible
In this lifetime.
We will experience the greater part of their maturation
In other lifetimes.

Horrible rebirths are extremely heavy,
So you must reject these things assertively.

Through reverted views
We see poorly.
We deviate from the correct path,
And we live as animals.
We droop downward when we move,
Or we live within the ocean,
And eat each other up.

Some are kept by people, and killed.
Some are disturbed by the waves,
And their abode is unreliable.
They have no refuge,
And are forever haunted by fear.

They are scattered about,
And live in unreliable places,
Such as among the nations of men.
They are boiled, seasoned, and sliced,
And are forced into multitudinous labors.

After they are made to experience many sorrows
They are slaughtered,

Advice to Kublai Khan

And we go to get their meat and other parts.
You can certainly see this.

Now the belly-crawlers are different.
For the most part,
The families that agree and the families that disagree
Are enemies,
And for this reason they are eternally afraid,
Until they reach the ends of their lives,
And they are tortured by so many sorrows.

The great nagas are also densely stupid.
They are usually afraid of fire, grains of sand, and garudas.
Consider well the way it is with them.
You must reject reverted views.

Hence, we must turn away from the ten non-virtues.
Moreover, we must totally shun
Anything that takes to the side of evil,
And when even a little should occur,
We confess it and avow ourselves,
To cleanse it completely.

Any deeds we do
That are motivated by non-attachment,
Non-hatred, and non-ignorance,
Will be helpful to others,
And bear a fruition of happiness.
These have been proclaimed to be virtues.

To turn others away from the work of murdering,
And to ransom the lives of those that are sure to die
Will help our bodies and our spirits.
We will live long and happy lives.

To turn others away from taking what is not given,
To delight in giving things to ourselves,
And to truly bestow what is needed on other beings
Will endow us with every glory and possession.

To turn others away from perverted desires,
And make them remember the grim prospects there are in attachments
So that they immerse themselves in pure Brahmanic behaviors

Will bring an absence of enemies, samadhi, and happiness.

When we turn others away from lying,
Reject the ways of contrivance,
And speak the truth,
We will not be deceived by other beings,
And we ourselves will be people of consequence.

When we turn others away from gossip,
Bring those who disagree into agreement,
And make agreements once again be stable,
We will have many friends,
And our lovers will be stable.

When we turn others away from random speech,
The time comes for we ourselves to be meaningful,
We will speak when the time is right
With a voice that is respected,
And our minds will also fall into their natural state.

When we turn others away from cruel words,
We ourselves speak pleasantly,
To make other beings joyful,
And we are praised by all the world.

When we turn others away from a covetous attitude,
We distribute our possessions liberally to others,
With a prayer that all their hopes will bear fruit.

When we turn others away from harmful attitudes,
We personally wish to help them,
And seriously endeavor to work for their benefit.
Then everyone will work to help us.

When we turn others away from reverted views,
We will immerse ourselves in a correct view,
We actually apply it to these others,
And we will carry on through a succession of happy lives.

These things mature as visible dharmas,
Yet we savor their experience only a little.
Their full maturation
Will be a ripening of these extraordinary things

Advice to Kublai Khan

Throughout our remaining lifetimes.

These are the ten acts of the karma of light.
We strive at all the karmas of virtue
Through their exemplification,
And we succeed in accomplishing them.
We also dedicate them to enlightenment,
So that we may help others,
So that they will not be exhausted, but prosper.

In this way the worldly may properly seek out the trails
Of happiness and sorrow, virtue and evil,
And practice along the way of a correct view.
We become brilliantly endowed with glories and wonders,
And we achieve the three happy lives
Of humans, asuras, and gods.

These virtues allow us to attain high status,
But they do not cut through the roots of this world,
And we will once again spin around in samsara.
We will not go on without further lifetimes.

If we examine these happy lives,
They are miserable.
We do not get what we want,
But lose it.
We do not get rid of what we don't want,
But meet with it.
The great, for the most part,
Have miserable minds.
The lowly, for the most part,
Have miserable bodies.
Human lives are entirely miserable.

To hate the glories of the gods,
And pass the time in argument,
Using the time available for battles:
This is how the asuras are defeated,
Both presently and in the future.

The gods decline
Due to transfer at death, downfall, having enemies, and carelessness,
Then they really do suffer in the lower abodes,

With birth, old age, sickness, and death.
These follow in concordance with the above.

There is suffering from pain,
Suffering from the loss of happiness,
And composite suffering.
All of them come from out of karma and emotional problems,
To torment all living things.

You must remember the sorrows of samsara in this way,
And train your mind to make a definite escape from them.
To do this,
I beg you to thoroughly tame your mind.

The mind is not something that has a form.
It is disturbed as it inquires,
And through the influences of what we are immersed in,
The mind contrives the mind.

Abandon those things
That make you develop emotional problems.
Brilliantly turn away from every disturbance.
This is how you must settle your mind in equanimity.

We turn away from the majority of our lusts
By looking at the impurity of flesh, fat, skin, and skeletons,
From hatred
By the waters of friendship,
From ignorance
By the path of dependencies and connections,
And from pride
By classifications according to domain.
These words were proclaimed by the Sage,
For these are the ways to smash emotional problems on the head.

We direct our minds using visualizations
Of gods, bodies, minds, and the rest.
Once we have settled our minds into equanimity,
We should start out with the meditation on peaceful abiding.

When we examine all these visualizations,
And all these dharmas,
They are like banana trees:

Advice to Kublai Khan

They are entirely empty of any essential truth.
This is the door to freedom.
It is described as: "Emptiness."

When something has no basis for definition
There is not the slightest thing to attach a definition to,
And our minds do not hold on to such things.
This is what it is to be undefined.

When there are no definitions,
there is nothing to be defined and nothing to attain,
So there is no attainment,
And there is nothing to pray for.
This is called: "Prayerlessness."

So it is that all Dharmas are, in their true essence,
Spontaneously formed,
So they are not truly compounded.
This is called: "The door to total freedom."

We must meditate on great compassion
For every living being that does not understand this.
This is how the compassion of emptiness
Works in every way
Toward the success of all our objectives,
And those of others.

Once we have entirely crossed over
These levels and paths,
We will be endowed with every wondrous thing,
And we will become truly perfected Buddhas,
The only friends for all sentient beings.

This is the heart-essence of the teachings of all the Buddhas.
It is unsurpassed.

Through what virtue there is in my presenting it
With words that are few but clear,
May I and all sentient beings,
Led by the prince that I am exhorting,
Very quickly attain unsurpassed enlightenment.

This fountain of the ambrosia of confidential advice was composed by the monk Phagpa to encourage the prince named Degus Bhoga in the male fire rat year (1276/77 A.D.) on the twenty fifth day of the month of the bangle. The secretary was Atsara. May it bring the highest good fortune.

ADVICE FOR KING HOKO

rGyal po ho ko la gdams pa

I bow to all the Buddhas and Bodhisattvas.

For the sake of Prince Hoko, I will speak a little on the ways in which the Dharma originated with the speech of the Buddha.

Now all these dharmas, including the world and the sentient beings within it, are not without causes. So they appear, but even this appearance is only for a little while. These things were not created by some creator that is single and permanent, be it a god such as Indra or Brahma, or be it something like the sky. We do not perceive that there is anything at all for such a creator to have made. Also, there are numerous dharmas to be created, so this singleness is not acceptable. All material things reach their completion gradually, so it is also not acceptable that they were created at one time. And if they were created gradually, then even their creator would turn out to be impermanent. For these reasons, there is no creator.

The source of the sentience of sentient beings is none other than our awareness, so there is nothing that hinders our minds. The source of our bodies is the four major elements. Now as for the act of bringing a body and a mind into synchronicity, and their happiness, sorrow, acquisitions, losses, and other details, these come about due to karmas that we have truly enacted in the past and due to temporary conditions. The vessel of the world supports the existence of these sentient beings, and is the basis of attachment, so it is the sky. Its source is the four major elements: earth, water, fire, and wind. These become joined and then are attached and held on to. The sentient beings who are to be born in it emerge by the force of their karma.

As for the way of this attachment, it begins with an attachment toward the foundation of condensed wind, which is extremely stable and is vast. On top of it, the wind moves, and this makes heat, and that which moves upwards then gathers into heaps of clouds, from which rivers of rain fall down. All this is based on the wind, and it abides as the lowermost ocean. This is where specks of gold become extremely hard, as if to form a crust. This is the foundation of mightiest gold.

On top of it, as before, a river of rain from the clouds falls. This is the external ocean. Within it there gather clumps of the dust of precious jewels, which form into Mt. Meru, the king of the mountains, and into seven golden mountains. In the four directions and their boundary areas there are four islands and eight sub-islands which are made from the dust of precious jewels and other compounded particles.

In the East there is Noble Body. To its left and right there are Body and Noble Body. These three are shaped as half-moons. In the South there is Jambu Island. To its left and right are Tail Father and Other Tail Father. These three are triangular. To the West there is Cow Pleasure. To its left and right are Motion and Supreme Path Motion. These three are round. In the North there is Unpleasant Sound. To its left and right there are Unpleasant Sound and Moon of Unpleasant Sound. These three are square.

Those are the twelve islands. In the areas between them there are a multitude of very small islands. This is the world of the humans. The higher reaches of the seven golden mountains and Mt. Meru is the abode of the asuras. The mandala of the wind, which swirls in a clockwise circle around the terraces of Mt. Meru and through the sky, is the abode of the four lines of great kings. At the top of Mt. Meru there is the abode of the Thirty Three. Above it there are a succession of very stable wind mandalas which form themselves into four levels of foundation that are made of precious things. This is the abode of the high gods of desire. On top of these there adhere, in the same manner, three more levels. These are the abodes of the first dhyāna meditation in the realm of form, and its thousands upon thousands of worlds are called: "General Development."[22] On the second thousands upon thousands there is the so-called: "Between Space."[23] The great thousand of three thousands upon thousands of such places is the so-called: "Domain of this World."

The domain of this world is intolerable. We take it to be level, but it is destructible.

The three levels that adhere right above the first dhyāna are the domain of the second dhyāna. The three levels that adhere above them are

[22] sPyi phud
[23] Bar ma

the abode of the third dhyāna. This is the vessel of the world, which is destructible. On top of it there is the abode for those in the fourth dhyāna. It adheres just outside the vessel of this world and it is not destructible. Our bodies appear there in synchronicity with a measureless private palace in which we abide and where we are destructible. It is also our practice ground. It is the sky.

The formless realm is where we have no bodies. It is not a place that transforms into something else.

Once we have attained the mind of samadhi, replacing the things we stopped doing in our previous life, we will be abiding in an unmoving state.

World realms like these are bountifully present throughout the ten directions, but we cannot be sure about whether they are great or small, or their form, of that they are there at the same time. Some of the world dominions have Mt. Meru and the four islands, and some of them do not have Mt. Meru and the four islands. Some of them are built upon the light of the sun and the moon. Some of them are built on the light from precious jewels. Some of them are built on the light of the Tathagata. They remain there in a variety of ways. These are the world vessels.

Upon becoming attached to these world vessels, the gods of the highest realms exhaust the karma they have for staying there, and are reborn in the realms of desire, descending in stages, while those who bring cessation to their minds through dhyāna meditation in stages exhaust their karma of desire, by which they were born in the realms of desire. It is by force of this that those to be born as males or females are born among the gods of the desire realms, the asuras, and human beings.

Then, when the time is right, sentient beings who live in other world dominions, who have gathered up the karma to be born in this one, become gods, asuras, children of the humans, or even animals and hungry spirits, right down to the wave-less hell.

There are four abodes of birth: Miraculous birth, birth from heat and moisture, birth from an egg, and birth from a womb.

Through the influence of non-virtues that are predominantly anger, we will be in hell. The hot sentient beings who dwell below this great earth are in hell. There are cold sentient beings in hell, and there are one day hells that are in a variety of abodes on top of the ground. They are touched by bounteous sorrows, for their environment is hot, cold, and hellish.

When desire is the major non-virtue, we become hungry spirits. They move below the earth, upon the earth, and in the sky, and are of two kinds: Those whose obstructions are external, and those whose obstructions are internal. They have many sorrows, thirst and hunger among them.

Through non-virtues that are primarily ignorance we become animals. Those who live in the great oceans or are scattered everywhere are dull and in darkness. They have terrible fear, and fall under the control of others. Nagas, as a species, are supreme. Most of them are well endowed. They are classed among the animals on account of their dullness and their fear of garudas.

These are the three horrible rebirths.

When our virtues are enmeshed with ignorance, we will be born human, and be divided among the twelve islands. There are those who live on the very minute islands, but they are brought together at whichever of the twelve islands they are near to. These humans are mostly full of thoughts about the Eight Dharmas of the world. Those who are very strong in mind are mostly happy, but it is fitting that they work consciously, so as not to fall under the control of sorrow. This is why the blessed Buddhas come forth from human lineage.

When our virtues are enmeshed in anger and jealousy we will be born as non-gods, as asuras. They have the same full store of endowments that the gods have, but they are slightly less fortunate, so they are called: "non-gods." They are angry about the endowments of the gods, so they pass their time fighting and arguing.

When our virtues are enmeshed in desire, we will become gods of desire, and move through the sky, as do the sun and moon, or we will be in the so-called Four Lines of Great Kings, who live in the terraces of Mt. Meru. The ones that live on top of Mt. Meru are the gods of the Thirty Three. These gods live with the fear of the non-gods. Above them there is freedom from war. The ones who live above them are the Joyful. They enjoy the bliss there is in the teachings of Lord Maitreya and others. The ones who live above them are in the Joy of Miracles. The ones who live above them take control of other's miracles. These are the six classes of the gods.

Their minds grow attached to the bliss of desire, so they are referred to as the Dominion of Desire.

We are born among the gods of the higher realms through karma that does not move. These are the stages of the gods who live above the gods that take control of other's miracles: The abode of Brahma, those that emerge in the presence of Brahma, and the Great Brahma. These three are the first dhyāna.

The real basis of these dhyānas, being associated with our thoughts and associated with our analytics, is a joy to develop in solitude, and it has a special bliss. This real basis is special, for it holds a samadhi in which we do not think, but simply analyze.

Then on top of them there are the abodes of the gods of three stages: Small Light, Measureless Light, and Clear Light. This is the second dhyāna. These are associated with joy, and employ a samadhi that is blissful.

Then on top of them, in three stages, are the abodes of the gods of Small Virtue, Measureless Virtue, and Vast Virtue. This is a samadhi that is without joy, but is blissful. This is the third dhyāna.

Then there are the abodes of the gods Cloudless, Propagating Merit, and Great Fruit. Then there are the abodes of the gods of Not Great, Untortured, Splendid Appearance, Highly Visible, and Nothing Less. These are the gods whose domain is the Abodes of Purity. Now these eight are subsumed into the fourth dhyāna. They have a samadhi that is an entirely pure equanimity, without thoughts of joy or bliss. Here, we have an extremely nice form, one that has the true nature of light, so this is called: "The form realm."

When we meditate in a way where the samadhi that represents the temporary conditions of our path is in the generative forces of the bounteous sky, the generative forces of bounteous consciousness, the generative forces that are nothing at all, and the generative forces that are neither existent nor non-existent, we will get the results of this, which are said to be that we attain the true peace of mind that these things support. The support for our minds has no form, so this is called: "The formless realm."

So it is that these vessels of worlds and their contents appear by force of dependencies and connections. The causes from the past, which material things take on of themselves, generate their essential fruition in the future. When previous conditions are brought together synchronously, they act to augment the special qualities of the result. This is called: "Occurrence through external dependencies and connections."

As for the way in which sentient beings come to be, our minds have no beginning, and the obstructions made by our habitual patterns also have no beginning. By their force we do not correctly understand our objects as they are. This is ignorance. By force of it we cling to objects as being permanent, solitary, and true, and we become attached to what is attractive. We despise what is unattractive. And so the rest of our emotional problems emerge. Being motivated by them we actually consolidate our karma of body, speech, and mind. This is consolidation. These two things are on the side of our lives in the past.

The awareness that makes us cross the borders through a womb or other means of birth is our consciousness. The composite of the five heaps is name and form. The development of internal generative powers, such as eyes, represents the six generative forces. When these internal generative forces contact an external object, there is touch. The experience of happiness and sorrow is feeling. Attachment to attractive objects is craving.

Our encompassing search to get what we desire is taking. By its power there will come a fruition, which is existence. These eight are in the present. Our old age and death in this life are subsumed into these.

Birth, here, refers to our transmigration into the future. When we have transmigrated, our future situations will mature and pass away. This is old age and death, so these two are in the future.

In this manner, the twelve branches are completed over three lifetimes. They can also be presented with cause and result occurring two times. Ignorance and consolidation are the causes of the present. The five that go from consciousness up to feeling are the results in the present. Craving, taking, and existence are causes for the future. Birth, old age, and death are results in the future. According to this method, the dependent and connected origination of results from the past turns out to be a cause for the future, so we have no certainty about any beginning or end. The wheel of samsara rolls on without stopping.

There is a fullness of the things that occur through dependencies and connections for sentient beings in the realm of desire. Those who are in the form or the formless are also complete in their dispositions.

The worlds that make up the vessels and their contents are subsumed into the heaps, the domains, and the generative forces. Now heaps are called this because they pile up. There are five: Form, feeling, perception, intention, and consciousness.

The heap of form is fitting for a form. It also has eleven parts: Eyes, ears, nose, tongue, body, form, voice, smell, taste, touch, and those things we do not thoroughly understand. This is spoken of in such sources as The Vows.

Feeling is experiencing. It also is of three sorts: Happiness, sorrow, and equanimity. This is what there is, but because they depend on things like eyes, there turns out to be six.

A perception is a grasping for a definition. There are also three kinds: The vast, the middling, and the small. These occur through a dependency on things like eyes, as well, so there are six.

Intentions are intentions to actually do something. There are two sorts: Intentions that come from our minds that are specific to our minds, and intentions that have no form, mind, or mental events.

Consciousness is a detailed understanding of an object. There are six kinds: Eye, ear, nose, tongue, body, and intellect.

Generative forces are the doors of birth for our consciousness. There are twelve: The generative forces of eye, ear, nose, tongue, body, intellect, and the generative forces of form, voice, smell, taste, touch, and dharma.

The domains signify the classes. There are eighteen: The eye structure and the rest of the six, the envisioned form and the rest of the six, and the consciousness that the eye supports and the rest of the six.

The generative forces of the dharmas, and the material things that make up their domain, are of seven kinds: Feelings, perceptions, intentions, and forms that are not understood in detail.

There are three things that are not compounded, and with the exception of these three uncompounded things, everything is compounded. Things that are not compounded are not generated out of causes and conditions. These are the three: The sky, the cessation through personal decision, which is to be obtained through wisdom, and the cessation which is not through personal decision, which will never occur while its conditions are incomplete.

Through an outline of one worldly domain we may also understand how it is with other worldly domains. The specifics on their dissimilarities have already been discussed above.

The world congeals through time without measure till it reaches a time of ten years, during which it declines, then there is a long period of increment, which grows till it reaches eighty thousand. Then it congeals again till it reaches ten. This is the turning point. This happens eighteen times, increasing into an amount without number then congealing for a long period of time. This will happen for twenty eons. Then the lifetimes of sentient beings will be done, they will be born into other world dominions, and this world will be emptied. The world vessel will be destroyed.

There are three conditions that make this destruction happen: Seven suns will rise, and their fire will destroy everything up to the first dhyāna. Water will cascade in rivers of rain from the clouds and destroy everything up to the second dhyāna. Then wind will destroy everything up to the third dhyāna. The duration of the destroying process is twenty eons. For twenty eons there is emptiness. The period of formation is also twenty eons. It abides for twenty eons. When there are eighty like this, it is called: "A great eon."

Now there are many ways and methods to liberate these worlds that congeal and destruct, along with the countless dominions of sentient beings in this great ocean of bountiful sorrow. There are those of gods such as Brahma and Indra. There are those of Rishis such as Paṇḍāra and Kaṇāda. There are the traditions of such people as Mishaha, Lab Gin, and Mahamad. These do not bring us to freedom from samsara. Their teachers have overall practices of attachment, hatred, and ignorance, for they have not gained freedom from samsara. The scripture traditions that hold their teachings are contradictory and contain many delusions. They do not turn out to be remedies for our emotional problems, which are the root of samsara.

The blessed Buddha is free from samsara's problems. He found the wisdom of omniscience. He truly engages himself in not being attached to his personal happiness and being a help to all sentient beings. There is nothing despicable in his activities, be they physical, verbal, or mental. The words of his orations do not, in the slightest, have the problems of being contradictory or delusional.

The way of the Dharma is of two sorts: The small vehicle and the great vehicle. The way of the small vehicle is for the classes that work to pacify the sorrows of samsara personally. They use the vows of personal freedom as a foundation, and turn away from the foundations of harmfulness and from doing harm to sentient beings. Based on these things, they work on the path of the four noble truths and the twelve ways that things occur in dependencies and connections.

Now the four noble truths are:

The truth of sorrow: We must know that the fruits of samsara are compounded, changing, and sorrowful, as is the world vessel where we live. It is like a disease.

The truth of the source is that we must get rid of samsara's causes, which are karma and emotional problems. They resemble the causes of a disease.

The truth of cessation is that when we terminate suffering and its causes we will abide in peace. We actually do this.

The truth of the path is the method by which we actually do this, and must be supported in our spirits, it being the path of this world and that goes beyond this world. This is like medicine.

This is primarily the path of the Auditors. I have already discussed samsara's causes and results, and its occurrence through dependencies and connections above.

Concerning the occurrence of nirvana through dependencies and connections, we comprehend dharmas individually and keep them in balance, so we understand our objects correctly, just as they are. This brings the cessation of ignorance and its friends, our emotional problems. Through this cessation our actions motivated by emotional problems do not consolidate, so there is the cessation of consolidation. Through this cessation, our consciousness does not transmigrate, so there is the cessation of consciousness. Through this cessation, we do not take on bodies, so there is the cessation of name and form. A foundation does not form, so specific dharmas will not be supported. This brings the cessation of the six generative forces. Through this cessation, we have no contact with external objects, so there is the cessation of touch. Through this cessation, we have no experience of an object, so there is the cessation of our external feelings.

Through this cessation, attachment to objects does not occur, so there is the cessation of craving. Through this cessation, we do not search in any way for desired things, so there is the cessation of taking. Through this cessation, a potency of causes will not occur, so old age and the destruction of the world do not occur, thus there is the cessation of death, sorrow, wailing, unhappy attitudes, and the rest, all the sorrows of the world, will not occur, and this is called: "Nirvana." This is of primary concern to those who are on the paths of Private Buddhas.

So it is that by meditating on the paths of the Auditors and Private Buddhas we will attain our first noble attitude, and enter the stream. No matter how we tarry, we will realize the fruition of Arhatship in seven lifetimes. Those who attain the fruition of Arhatship after being born once in the realms of desire are the once-returners. Those who attain the fruition of Arhatship while in the same realm as mentioned above are the non-returners. Those who make it to the end of their five paths while in this very body are Arhats who do not take rebirth. Now there are two aspects to each of these, in terms of how we engage in them and how we abide in their fruition, and so it is that there are eight kinds of noble person.

There are three kinds of Arhat: Auditor Arhats, Private Buddha Arhats, and Buddha Arhats. In all three of them we have a nirvana in which our heaps continue, for so long as we have not yet relinquished our heaps. Once we are free from these closely held heaps, our minds are truly at peace. This is nirvana in which our heaps do not continue.

They believe that this is the final fruition. These are what we call: "The ways of the small vehicle."

The way of the Mahayana has three parts: Our cause, our path, and our fruition.

Our cause is our minds. The natural purity of our minds is our innate heritage. When we use great compassion to develop our minds toward supreme enlightenment this is called our developed heritage. That is our cause.

In preparation for the path, we go for refuge. The cause of great compassion is our motivation. Our objects are the Buddha, the Dharma, and the Sangha. The time is for so long it may take until we ourselves are enlightened. The way is that the Buddha is our teacher, the Dharma is our path, and the Sangha are our friends. Once we have gone for refuge we have embarked upon the trail of the Three Jewels.

The actual path is of two kinds:

When our thoughts cultivate an attitude of supreme enlightenment we have a friendliness that is a wish that every sentient being right up to the end of the sky may meet with happiness, and a compassion that is a wish that they be free from every sorrow. We are motivated by thinking about a wish to attain Buddhahood so that we can help them. Then we take a vow in our thoughts: "I will attain the status of a Buddha." This is called the cultivation of a wishful enlightened attitude.

When we take a vow to put all the Buddha's paths and techniques into practice, this is the development of an engaged attitude toward supreme enlightenment. To make it ultimate, we develop great compassion, for every sentient being has been our father, mother, and child throughout beginningless samsara. We recollect the grim prospects there are in both samsara and nirvana. We recollect the virtues of the Buddha. We must grow accustomed to four kinds of consciousness we begin to experience when we make our promise before the Buddhas and Bodhisattvas.

Second, the application of this. There is our view, our practice, and our meditation.

Our view is that the heaps, domains, and generative forces, which were presented above, and every Dharma that may be subsumed within the path and its fruition, are obscured, and appear to us like dreams, like illusions. The ultimately true nature of all these things is that they are not complicated, like the sky. We must know and integrate these things.

Second, our practice is of two kinds: That which we do to complete our own objectives, and the six perfections that we do to achieve the objectives of sentient beings.

To give away all that we harbor is generosity. When we classify it, generosity is of four kinds: Material things, fearlessness, Dharma, and friendship.

To give up everything that does not accommodate our path is the rule of the way. When we classify it, the rule of the way is of three kinds: The rule of the way by which we vow to shun evil, the rule of the way by which we consolidate the Dharmas of virtue by working steadfastly toward virtue, and the rule of the way by which we work to the extent of our ability to help sentient beings, directly or indirectly.

Not shifting our minds toward things that do not accommodate our path is patience. When we classify it, there are three kinds: To take sorrow seriously, to tolerate no torment, and to have a sure mind about the Dharma.

To work steadfastly toward success on the path is perseverance. When we classify it, there are two sorts: Perseverance that is armor in our quest for virtue, and perseverance where we apply our bodies, voices, and minds toward success at this quest.

To settle our minds one-pointedly is dhyāna meditation. When we classify it, it is of two kinds: The samadhi of rejection, in which we pacify uncomfortable positions, and the samadhi in which we work to make the wonders we are to attain into something real.

The knowledge of objects just as they are is wisdom. When we classify it, there two kinds: Obscured knowledge, which is an understanding of the individual causes and results that make up a subject as occurring through dependencies and connections, and ultimate knowledge, which is that the reality of these things is not complicated.

Second, the four real things that we organize toward a thorough maturation of sentient beings are: We organize sentient beings, we organize material things by distributing any requisites we may have in an effort to organize a temporary happiness for them, we organize opportunities to hear the teaching of the Dharma of the six perfections, and we organize to engage in their significance, we engage ourselves in practicing the things we have heard.

The organizing we do through harmonious objectives is where we engage in a personal behavior that is in harmony with these ways, so that those we must train may believe them.

Third, there is meditation.

When we meditate on friendship and compassion, our objects are sentient beings. When we meditate on faith our objects are our guru and the Precious Ones. The yidam deities and such things involve visualization. Once we understand that the objects we meditate on are appearances that lack any true nature, that they are like images in a mirror, we settle our minds into one-pointed equanimity. This is a samadhi that has no visualizations. It is peaceful abiding.

After we have meditated in these ways, we analyze these ways of meditation individually, till the meditation and the thing we meditate on have no unity or plurality. This will turn out to be a samadhi that has no visualizations or cravings. This is higher perception.

Meditation is the inter-connection between peaceful abiding and higher perception.

When we work strenuously in the ways of the view, practice, and meditation, we will attain a noble attitude, so we will largely accumulate merit and wisdom. This is called: "The path of accumulation."

After this, we immerse ourselves completely in samadhi, so we acquire supernatural cognitions and a power over miracles, which are of the world, and we acquire an attitude that will bring us into contact with the wisdom that is beyond this world. This is called: "The path of application."

At the end of this we see that the natural state of every dharma is not complicated. This is called: "The path of seeing."

We meditate on the unique significance of what we see, and immerse ourselves in it, so our noble virtues grow higher and higher. This is called: "The path of meditation."

Now if we divide these according to our stages of understanding, there are ten levels.

When we give birth to the wisdom of the path of seeing we attain a noble attitude and take joy in it. This is Total Joy. In a single instant we miraculously travel to one hundred Buddha fields. We traverse a hundred of the world's dominions. We see the faces of a hundred Buddhas. We receive a hundred different kinds of blessings from them. We achieve a hundred different kinds of samadhi and engage ourselves in them. We use a hundred different bodies to teach a hundred different Dharmas to a hundred different sentient beings, and we bring them to maturity. We live for a hundred eons. We know the past and future limits of a hundred eons. We attain thirteen hundred wondrous virtues.

After this we will attain the rule of the way of the blissful Buddhas, the second level, the Stainless. We attain all those previous wonders, multiplied a thousand times.

After this we will become illuminators of the transmitted Dharma, the third level, Light Maker. We attain all those previous wonders, multiplied a hundred thousand times.

After this we are endowed with the holy Dharma of understanding, the fourth level, Effulgent Light. We attain all those previous wonders, multiplied by a hundred ten millions.

After this we are endowed with the power to work to help sentient beings who are difficult to train, the fifth level, Difficult Study. We attain all those previous wonders, multiplied by a thousand ten millions.

After this we correctly understand the obscured and the ultimate, so we realize both the Dharmas of samsara and those of nirvana, the sixth level, Realization. We attain all those previous wonders, multiplied by a hundred thousand ten millions.

After this most of our mental disturbances and their symptoms will be cleansed, and we embark on the path of unified traversing, the seventh level, Far Gone. We attain all those previous wonders, multiplied by a hundred thousand million ten millions.

After this we become free from every symptomatic disturbance, and we are empowered into our objective to understand all Dharmas in their equality, the eighth level, the Undisturbed. We attain all those previous wonders, multiplied to equal the minute atoms that make up a hundred thousand world dominions.

After this we are endowed with empowerment into four separate and correct understandings: The meaning, the Dharma, the words, and the audacity, so we become important people who profess the Dharma, the ninth level, Excellent Intellect. We attain all those previous wonders, multiplied to equal the minute atoms that make up ten hundred thousand world dominions.

After this we are endowed with empowerments into samadhi and through the doors of spells, and nothing hinders our exhibition of manifest bodies or our unblocked access to the Dharma's gates, the tenth level, Cloud of Dharma. We attain all these previous wonders, multiplied to equal the atoms in all the bounteous worlds.

This is the path of meditation.

After this we use the vajra-like samadhi to overcome our obstructions right at the root, along with our habitual patterns, and we make our fruition into something real. This is the path that goes to the end.

These are the paths of the Mahayana.

When we purify our obstructions, both our emotional problems and the things that we must know, along with our habitual patterns, it is like clouds dispersing from the sky. Our dominion and our wisdom are of one flavor. This is called: "The body of the Dharma." Our hearts do not depart from the dominion of the Dharma, while the power of our merit and prayers from of yore bring us into the pure land of Dense Array in Akaniṣṭa, which is a practice ground exclusively for the noble. We have thirty-two fine physical markings, and eighty exemplary features. Our voices have sixty cadences.

All the inexhaustible Dharmas appear to us like mirror images in our hearts, which is the wisdom that resembles a mirror. When our hearts are balanced with regard to samsara and nirvana we have the wisdom of equanimity. When we know each individual subject in total perfection, and do not mix them up, we have the wisdom to discern specifics. When we work to fulfill the objectives of sentient beings while we have no thoughts, we have the wisdom to get things done. When we integrate the dominion of the Dharma into our hearts without complicating it, we have the wisdom of the dominion of the Dharma.

The teacher of the Mahayana Dharma remains forever without passing into nirvana and is embodied in perfect pleasure, teaching exclusively for Bodhisattvas on the tenth level who have the five wisdoms. The initiative of this embodiment as perfect pleasure is to appear in the minds of everyone among the bounteous dominions of sentient beings just as it wishes, to work to help these sentient beings. These are manifest embodiments.

This is how Buddhas, who do have these three embodiments and five wisdoms, do remain for so long as there is samsara, working for the welfare of sentient beings. This is the fruition of the Mahayana.

So I have spoken a little to present this outline of the Dharmas of the small and great vehicles.

This is for Prince Hoko. Phagpa composed it at Shing Kun during the fifth month of the male water monkey year (1272/73 A.D.). The secretary was Atsara.

TALKING ABOUT SHAME
FOR BAD WAYS OF PRACTICE

Ngan pa'i spyod tshul la khrel pa'i gtam

I am speaking out here:

During these corrupt times
Our way is in a state of corruption.
We are totally sliding
Down the road of corruption.
This is what these ways of thought and practice,
Which are in fact corrupt,
Look like:

I want to be happy,
And everyone else wants to be happy,
Yet we fail to engage our intellects
In the treasuries of the Sugata's orations,
Which are fountains of happiness.
I consider such ways to be embarrassing.

We have come into a perfect store of wonder:
The leisure and opportunity of being human.
Companions in virtue have taken us on their trails.
Yet we don't work to succeed at anything of much significance,
And then later on we shoot off prayers.
I consider such ways to be embarrassing.

Chogyal Phagpa

We have gone for refuge
With gurus who make the achievement of supreme bliss easy,
And we support them,
But we don't strive to do anything good with what they tell us.
I consider such ways to be embarrassing.

There are those who solicit their gurus mentally,
But use their bodies and words in a hundred ten million ways
To ridicule the hearts of the ones who actually teach them.
I consider such ways to be embarrassing.

There are those who are lovingly gifted
With the heart-blood of words of instruction,
But then ask: "What else is there that we can work on?"
I consider such ways to be embarrassing.

There are those who do not strive to make offerings
To these oceans of wonder,
And do not concern themselves with the meaning
Of what the lord of the two-footed has said,
But hope they will get something good out of them personally.
I consider such ways to be embarrassing.

There are those who fail to get on the trails
Of the ones with the best intellects,
And surely contradict the words of the holy ones,
While they hope that all their personal goals will be realized.
I consider such ways to be embarrassing.

There are those who constantly evade and flee from holy ones,
While they extend courtesies to mean people,
Hoping that their own licentious behavior will look beautiful.
I consider such ways to be embarrassing.

There are those who fail to engage their intellects
In the profound and vast spoken words that are dependable
With regard to the meaning of the meditation we must do,
While hoping to be liberated just because they meditate.
I consider such ways to be embarrassing.

There are those who are capable of success,
But fail to succeed at anything of great significance,
While they say: "I don't succeed because I am very lazy."

Advice to Kublai Khan

They boast about their faults as if they were virtues.
I consider such ways to be embarrassing.

May these people who get tied up in the yarn of perverse desires,
And are delighted with evil rebirths,
Be endowed with heroic minds that keep to the way,
And may they move on toward behaving like holy people.

I am speaking out here
For the maintenance of our way of practice,
For I have seen how our way is in a state of schism.
So I, a bearer of the glorious banner of the intelligence of the holy ones,
Have, in an effort to turn things around, composed this
In the fire snake (1257/58 A.D.) during the month of the king.

THE HEART ESSENCE
OF THE PATH TO ENLIGHTENMENT

Byang chub lam gyi snying po

I bow to all the Buddhas and Bodhisattvas.

Now, for those who have their wits, there are two ways to work toward achieving unexcelled enlightenment:

Those who are extremely diligent will quickly achieve Buddhahood through difficult practices, while those who are wise with regard to methods will gradually achieve Buddhahood by engaging in what they enjoy and revere. On this point, the Sutra called The Perfect Appearance of the Tathagata says:[24]

The Blessed One made a statement: "Ananda, I used blazing diligence to quickly achieve a fully perfect enlightenment, and became a truly perfect Buddha. I felt pain, torture, and abuse. These are the ways I achieved fully perfect enlightenment and became a truly perfect Buddha."

He also said: "Ananda, a Bodhisattva Mahasattva who uses friendship for a practice of Bodhisattva activity will be wise in his methods, and will finish with everything. This vehicle is a happy one. It is comfortable to engage in it. Use this path of happiness and you will succeed, as is proper, in achieving fully perfected enlightenment."

---

[24] De bzhin gshegs pa yang dag par 'byung ba

So it is that there are two ways. Now here I will be talking about the way to achieve enlightenment through engaging in happiness.

There are three Dharmas that we must understand:

The way of the preliminaries, which entails complications,
The actual practice, in which we place ourselves in equanimity, and is not complicated,
And the avenues of the path, which bring us to fulfillment.

For the first of these, we set out any offerings we may possess in a secluded place, in the visible presence of the Precious Ones, three times by day and three times by night. Then we take refuge in our gurus and the Three Jewels, three times.

We must attain Buddhahood for the sake of all sentient beings. This is the function of the avenues of enlightenment. We use the Seven Branches as a preliminary to engender an enlightened attitude, which is precious, motivating ourselves with the consideration, in our thoughts, that we will assiduously work toward success in this to the extent of our ability. We plant the fore of our right knee on the ground and lodge our religious garment over one of our shoulders. Then we join our palms, either at our hearts or at the crown of our heads, toward the sky before us, where our guru, our companion in virtue, sits there smiling, and there on a lion throne right in front of the Bodhi tree, the Blessed Buddhas who presently live and thrive throughout all the bounteous and brilliantly diversified realms in the ten directions of our world, who know all the Dharmas and see every sentient being, who have relinquished pretentions and anxieties in their guardianship of sentient beings, sit there as a refuge that is palpable, obvious, and distinct. They have made the Dharma that we are to actually understand into something real, and speak out the vast and profound transmissions of the Dharma. He is surrounded by an oceanic assembly of Bodhisattvas and a Sangha of auditors. We visualize all of them, in all their numbers, as if they were actually there, our minds settled into an equanimity of recollection.

Then, there in the visible presence of each of them, there are arraigned, in a unified company, all the sentient beings that there are, equal to the ends of the sky, their bodies made manifest in numbers equal to the most minute atoms that make up the nations of the world. All of them join their hands, bowing to the Buddhas and their retinues. They go for refuge for the duration, until they reach the heart of enlightenment, and present massive clouds of offerings, as if they were magical manifestations of total goodness. Then we join with these manifest beings in offering our own bodies, possessions, and every root of virtue that we have gathered from throughout the three times. We confess all of our own evils, and those of every sentient being. To the extent of our ability, we take on our vows once again. We rejoice in every root of virtue, be it of samsara with its ten directions and three times, or of nirvana. We encourage all the blessed Buddhas who dwell in the bountiful worlds of the ten directions to turn the wheel of the profound and vast Dharma. We request that they remain in the world for as long as it exists, without passing into nirvana, and work to help sentient beings.

Then these blessed Buddhas, for the sake of sentient beings, engender an enlightened heart and employ themselves in every enlightened activity that will bring us to full completion, and just as they have employed themselves, once they had actually finished becoming Buddhas, at helping sentient beings, we too now engender the enlightened attitude that we will do this for the sake of all sentient beings.

We will study every path towards enlightenment, according to procedure, and we vow that once we have actually finished becoming Buddhas we will work toward helping every sentient being that has not already been liberated by the Victorious Ones of the past.

With these considerations in our thoughts, we should speak out these words:

> O Gurus,
> Companions in Virtue,
> You whose compassion preserves knowledge,
> You have taken me, and these others, on your trail,
> And taught us the profound path.
> You have made it possible for us to succeed
> In the efforts of all the Buddhas.
> I bow to you.
>
> I will bow forever with a respectful attitude
> To my holy gurus,
> For they maintain the true heart
> Of all the Buddhas of the three times,
> And are joined in a lineage,
> To all the Buddhas,
> Foremost among the two-footed,
> For they abide throughout the three times and ten directions,
> To the Dharma,

And to the noble Sangha.

I come to you as a true refuge,
Until I am enlightened,
For you shelter me from every inhospitable condition.
I will become someone who is like you,
So please bless me in all things.

I offer you noble ones who dwell in the sky,
And in the worlds that fill the dominion of the sky,
My body, possessions, virtues,
And oceanic clouds of offerings
Which I have made manifest with my mind.
May they satisfy everyone that lives.

I confess each one of the evils that I,
And all these bounteous sentient beings, none excepted,
Have committed, physically, verbally, or mentally,
While under the control of our karma
And the proclivities of our emotional problems.
Please grant that they be made pure.

I rejoice in any virtues there may be
In every world throughout the three times and ten directions,
However many there may be.
May everyone alive also rejoice in each other,
So that our virtues may be augmented.

I now come before all you Victorious Ones,
In cooperation with everyone that is living,
To respectfully present a request
That you teach the Dharma,
And remain here to work forever to help sentient beings,
Without passing away into nirvana.

Just as the Victorious Ones achieved greatness
Through propagating a heart of enlightenment,
And worked to help those who live,
So too do I propagate an enlightened attitude,
And will learn these practices according to procedure.

We should recite this from our deepest marrow, the core of our bones, till we have done it three or seven times.

Next, we sit with our legs folded on a comfortable mat, in whatever way is comfortable. We relax for a little bit. Then, we should recollect on the meaning of these Seven Branches that we have just recited in the above.

Then we should recollect, in a proper series, on the grim prospects there are in samsara and in nirvana, on friendship, on compassion, on enlightened attitudes that are wishful, applicable, and the ultimate, on the nature of the path in which emptiness and compassion are interactive, on the perfect Buddhahood that is its fruition, on its wondrous qualities, and on the propagation of its good works. We start out at the beginning and go on to the end.

Then we consider this series from the end back to the beginning, contemplating which things are based on which other things, and in particular, we dwell on those topics that we revere and that are therapeutic for our minds. Once we have done this recollection, we place ourselves in equanimity.

These are the techniques of the preliminaries, inclusive of their complications.

Next there is the actual practice, in which we place ourselves in a state of equanimity in which there are no complications. This can be done either right after we do the Seven Branches, or at some other time.

We cross our two legs on a comfortable mat. We position our two hands on a level. We keep our spine straight. We set our eyes on the tip of our noses. We go to our gurus and the Three Jewels for our refuge. We meditate on an enlightened attitude, as it has been explained to us. Then we visualize that our own body instantaneously turns into our Yidam deity. It has no true nature. It is like an image in a mirror. Our own guru sits on the crown of our heads, in the style of the lord of our lineage. We do this meditation with a fierce reverence and respectfulness. Then we present a solicitation, saying: "Please propagate correct understanding in my spirit, and the holy samadhi that will settle me into the wisdom of total liberation."

Then we focus on things that are outside us and inside us, just as they appear and just as we experience them. All these things appear to our minds without attribution, and we experience them, but on careful analysis they have no unity or plurality. So it is that they appear to us while they lack any true nature, as if they were dreams. When we then focus on these things that appear to us in these ways, we see that it is from out of our minds, which are removed from virtue, non-virtue, conclusions, or perspectives, that the totality of happiness, sorrow, samsara, and nirvana appears. So it is that the root or basis of all things is our mind.

If we then investigate this mind, it is not made out of colors and shapes. It lacks unity and plurality. It dwells neither outside nor inside us, and is not in both of them. For these reasons it is empty of a private essentiality.[25] Anything that lacks essentiality is empty of any cause that would make it occur, and something that does not occur does not remain. So it is also empty of any essentiality which might remain for the meanwhile. Something that does not remain does not cease, so it is also empty of any result that might be a final conclusion. Something that has no beginning or end, and lacks essence, has nothing whatever about it that might be designated to be a boundary or center, so it is entirely free from the three times. Something that lacks boundaries and a center is also entirely free from all complications. This is the reality of the mind. This is also the true nature of all things. This is, in fact, what is essential about the Buddha's embodiment as the Dharma.

So it is that we cut through complications. We do not hold onto definitions that involve the existence or absence of anything. We settle ourselves in equanimity, in a state that is free from complications.

Now, at first there will be a time during which we are not acclimatized to this, where we will fall into the extremes of realism and nihilism, and there will occur a multitude of mental abridgements and extrapolations, but there will come a time in which we have become acclimatized. Our inner mind will be clear. Our awareness and external appearances will both be freed from definitions and conceptualizations, as if in an unbroken stream. This understanding will give birth to a holy samadhi in our spirits that is not complicated. This river of samadhi is born out of our store of merit and wisdom. When we see this, we will get rid of the shadows that we must relinquish and we will propagate a wisdom regarding the path on which we can see what is beyond this world.

When we arise from this samadhi in which we have placed ourselves in equanimity, we will have extreme compassion for all those sentient beings who do not understand the way of it, and we will meditate on great compassion, thinking: "What would be wrong about it if they got

---

[25] Rang gi ngo bo

rid of the darkness of ignorance and all their karma and emotional problems, and became free from all their pain?"

Then we do a contemplation in which we think: "Through all my virtues, and those of others, the foremost of which are the roots of virtue that come from the meditation on this yoga of placing ourselves in equanimity, as our actual practice, and the Seven Branches that precede it, may all sentient beings truly become perfect Buddhas." Then we should say this three times:

> I will use my mind to combine these virtues,
> With every other root of virtue there may be,
> Into a unity,
> So may I and all these sentient beings,
> Equal to the sky,
> Attain unexcelled perfect enlightenment.

Then we imagine that our gurus, and all those others that we had imagined were in the sky before us, depart for their own abodes. Then we do whatever makes us happy.

That is the yoga that we actually practice.

Now for the avenues of the path, which bring these three topics to conclusion:

We will personally avoid evil and non-virtuous karma. If we should have a downfall, and do something evil, we follow up by recollecting the Buddhas of the ten directions, and we confess. We persevere in working to develop roots of virtue, to the extent of our ability. We dedicate all the virtues we have done toward an enlightenment than which there is no higher, so that we may help other beings. These other beings, in turn, will turn away from evil, and if they should be stained by any evil, we encourage them to confess it. We encourage them toward virtue, and to dedicate themselves toward that enlightenment than which there is no higher. We then meditate constantly on friendship, which is a wish for all sentient beings that they meet up with happiness; on compassion, which is a wish that they be freed from sorrow; and on an enlightened attitude, which is the thought: "May I and all sentient beings rapidly become Buddhas." We contemplate that everything that seems to appear outside of us is like an illusion, that everything our minds experience that seems to be inside of us is like a dream, and that the natural reality of all these things does not constitute the essential presence of anything, but is free from complications, like the sky.

At times when we experience physical and mental pains, we meditate on joy, which is the thought that the evils we have accumulated in the past are being purified. We meditate on the thought: "Through the pain that I experience may I reach out to the pains of all sentient beings, and may they be exhausted." We should not be depressed or docile. At times when we have happiness and joy in our bodies and minds, we follow up with a recollection of the wondrous benefits there are in virtue, thinking: "All of this happiness and joy, and the most excellent happiness and joy that are even greater than this happiness, comes about through the practice of virtue." Then we make a further recollection on the kindness there is in our purpose, thinking: "These practices of virtue have come to us through the support of our gurus and the precious ones." Then we follow up with contemplation, thinking: "May all sentient beings have an unbroken stream of joy and happiness that is like this and is even better than it." Then we train ourselves so that this basis of happiness does not become a mental addiction or some kind of arrogance.

These are the avenues of the path.

So it is that this yoga in which we constantly integrate these three Dharmas is pleasant to engage in and is an easy technique for gradually traversing the path of enlightenment. We actually employ all the joy and happiness that there is in this world and what is beyond this world, and in the end we actually become truly perfect Buddhas in that fully perfected enlightenment than which there is no higher.

> So it is that my students have urged me to explain
> The ways of meditating on
> The Heart Essence of the Path to Enlightenment
> In keeping with the transmission and the upadeśa.
> Through the virtue there is in this
> May everyone alive become a perfect Buddha.

This so-called Stages of Meditation on the Heart Essence of the Path to Enlightenment was quickly composed at the presentation of requests by my students who are far away by the monk Phagpa in the year of the male earth tiger (1279/79 A.D.), on the twenty-second day of the month of the bangle at the grand Dharma School of Pal Sakya.

Advice to Kublai Khan

THE WAY TO RESTORE MEMORY

Dran pa gso tshul la bstan pa

Oṃ Svasti Siddhaṃ

O Gurus for those who live,
You have filled your stores of merit and wisdom,
And thrown your faults and the things that cause them far away.
You have completely perfected your every wondrous quality.
I bow to your feet.

My guru is the very best of guides.
He uses kindness to set me free
From all the things that shackle my perspective.
He shows me the path of magnificent happiness.
He protects me from all the terrors of this world
And of its pacification.
I bow to his feet.

My companion in virtue is the best.
He has gathered the precious jewels of good upadeśa
From out of the ocean of the Victorious One's well compiled orations,
And he has given them to me truly.
I must remember them and write down his technique.

This world is an ocean of sorrow.
It is totally packed with the crocodile consortiums
That are our emotional problems.

It is totally wrecked
By waves of birth, aging, illness, and death.
There is no beginning to this.
There is no end.
It has no boundaries.
It has no center.
It does not diminish.
It does not grow.

From time with no beginning
We have been wandering around in such a sea.
If we go on like this,
And fail to turn back the tide,
We will wander on,
Without ever reaching a future ending.
So we must now persevere,
And sever its course.

There are teachers who are not free from the shackles of this world.
There are teachings that do not countermand the cause of this world.
There are companions in virtue who concern themselves with consummate worldliness.
Those who follow their trails might leave them totally behind,
But, being congenitally blind, are like people who set out to sea with no friends.

There are teachers who are faultless and whose wondrous qualities are complete.
There are teachings that are real remedies for selfish perspectives.
There are companions in virtue who are most wise
Regarding the path of decisive revulsion.
Those who wish to ford through this world depend on them.
They climb aboard a magnificent ship
Whose captain is the very best.
They cross over this vast ocean,
And land on jeweled isles.
They are like wish-fulfilling jewels
Who succeed at helping themselves and others.

This was narrated by Phagpa.

Advice to Kublai Khan

A LETTER TO ATSARA

A tsa ra la spring ba

You are a man who has achieved
Leisure and opportunity.
You have entered the door of the ambrosial teachings.
You have taken vows for good austerities.
You understand what must be taken on
And what must be relinquished,

But if you do not persevere at yoga,
On account of this life's happiness,
Or repute,
Or a lack of heart,
Or for fame,
Your austerities will fail.
Who in the three worlds
Is a greater fool than this?

You have perfect stores,
But do not cling to this happiness.
Do not quit your yoga
For the sake of these things.

When you have emotional problems,
Recollect your training.
How could you not know that it is holy?

You know only the way of these things
According to tradition,
But do not be content to be satisfied with this.
You must practice these things
Over and over.
Accustom yourself to meditation
To replenish your inner being.

When you experience happiness,
Give it to others.
When you experience sorrow,
Bear it for the sake of others.
When you are equanimous,
Place yourself in the equanimity of peace.
Work assiduously on these three ways of the Dharma.
Take your previous vows into your experience,
And keep them!

I have been listening,
And am sure you have the mental power.
This being sure,
Do not go adrift from this advice,
Offered out of love,
For it endows you with knowledge.

Now in the package with these comprehensive instructions
I give you fifty ambrosia tablets.
Offer them to all the Victorious One's mandalas,
Outer and inner,
And receive the eternal siddhis!

I wrote this letter in the female iron sheep year (1271-72 A.D.), on the twenty-seventh day of the month of offering, during the evening, at the castle of Shingkun. May it bring good fortune.

This is the letter of advice to Atsara.

AN EXCELLENT WORK OF ADVICE FOR THE KING

rGyal po la gdams pa'i rab tu byed pa

I bow to all the Buddhas and Bodhisattvas.

After bowing to the supreme glory of the Buddha,
Glorifying him in words of fame and renown,
For his glory in the miraculous intent of his virtues,
I will present this unto the glory of our holy ruler.

Bend down and listen to this exposition
Of the two kinds of classics.
You have seen them in your heart,
And have become engaged in them,
But as it is with the songs of musicians
And the instruments they play,
Why shouldn't poets take them up once again?

The Sage has proclaimed innumerable heaps of the Dharma,
So that he might help his abundant disciples.
All of them are sources to be taken into our experience,
And nothing more.
So you must know their ways as follows.

People in fear and those bound by shame
Do not break the laws made by the king.

Just so, those who live in keeping with the way
Augment their glory without harm,
And are praised, even by the king.

In order to keep track of beginners who have karma,
The Sage made rules that are common among the vehicles.
We take them up according to our own ability to practice them,
Using rituals complete in their branches,

So that both those who are terrified
By the sorrows of the world,
Visible and invisible,
And the hosts of noble ones who see the other side,
Might work things out in their hearts.

We are bound by shame,
And we guard ourselves in keeping with the way.
This is the basis for happiness in this world,
Both visible and invisible,
And for all the wonders of total freedom.
We become worthy of the offerings of gods and humans,
And we are praised,
Even by the Buddhas.

These three worlds are nothing but sorrow.
Nirvana is also nothing but peace.
So we look at samsara and nirvana
As objects of compassion,
And pray for them.

The Buddha is the only one
Who has no sorrow and removes every sorrow,
Who has found great happiness and seeks out happiness for everyone.

What is more,
He was someone like me.
His methods made him able to succeed.
That is why I too will surely attain Buddhahood.

We must meditate on the highest enlightened attitude
Without apprehension,
Without a casual attitude,
And without deceit.

When we transgress them we will burn in hell.
There is happiness in keeping them.
We will immediately attain a miraculous fruition of happiness.
Once we have taken on samaya,
We must guard them as dearly as our lives.

So it is that there are three vows for the three vehicles.
They are the basis for the development, maintenance, and prosperity
Of all our wondrous virtues,
And those of others.
I recommend that we depend on them
At the very beginning.

We must ascertain the specifics of the Dharma
Through the Dharma,
For its words are entirely filthless.
It is thoroughly ascertained through two kinds of validation.
It is not contradictory,
And it is virtuous at the beginning, in the middle, and at the end.

Its speaker has unhindered genius.
He does not covet his books,
But teaches them.
He has love.
He removes the problems there are in positions that disagree.
He knows about the acquisition of great power.
He is a Buddha.

They follow his trail.
Their virtue is a concordant cause for what they are.
They are the finest community.
They share their practice fields.
We ascertain that their field is holy,
For they gather in virtue.

They teach us truly,
Bring boundaries together,
Have the accoutrements of three kinds of virtue,
And kindly contemplate protecting us.
We must be constantly stable in our meditation
On a non-divisive faith in our gurus.

For those whose true nature it is
To hold to the stream of the cause and the essence,
Just as we wish to be free ourselves from sorrow and its cause,
So does every living being without exception want to be free.
We meditate on great compassion for them,
So they are not stolen.

We recollect the benefits there are
In the virtues of caring for supreme enlightenment,
For the welfare of others,
And for our temporary objectives,
And we practice them.
We apply ourselves to this everywhere
With a fierce resolve.

So it is that faith, compassion, and a longing attitude
Are preliminaries for all our works.
We use even the slightest element of virtue
To be motivated and to practice.

We look at bodies that are before us,
Or our own,
As being embodiments of the physique of the lord of sages.
Our place is a Buddha Field.
Everyone who is born and is alive
We make out to be a Buddha,
A child of the Buddha,
Or a student.
We use an ocean of gift-clouds
To make offerings to ourselves and others
Of all the pleasures that are the objects our five senses.

Once we are aware that our guru and all the Victorious Ones,
Without exception,
Are essentially the same in their form and good works,
And that there is no duality,
We contemplate at all times that they are before us,
Are at the crown of our heads,
Or that they sit in the center of the lily of our hearts,
And we present them our requests,
Or we meditate that there is no duality.

Advice to Kublai Khan

The root of all the dharmas:
Virtue, evil, happiness, sorrow,
Likewise, samsara and nirvana,
Is our minds.

When we make a thorough investigation of our mind,
In every way,
We see that it is not a color.
It is also not a shape.
It is not one.
It is not many.
For these reasons it is not an essence,
And therefore is not born.
It does not stay.
It does not stop.
It has no borders or center.
Its way of being is the uncomplicated sky.

While this is so,
Our awareness does not stop.
This is the identity of awareness and emptiness.

The way it is with my mind
Is likewise the nature of the mind
For every sentient being,
And all the dharmas are also
An interaction of appearance and emptiness.
We ascertain this comprehensively,
And use a way in which we do not grasp
To settle ourselves into intense equanimity.

So we place ourselves into equanimity
In two ways that use visualizations,
Without visualizations,
And in a state of interaction,
So that without being pushed around by our ideas,
We come to attain the holy samadhi
Of peaceful abiding.

We must repeatedly recollect the joy
That follows all our deeds,
Whether virtuous or evil,
And recall the virtuous,

So that we may augment its power
And make it increase.

After we have settled ourselves
Into a specific visualization,
We scrutinize the visualization,
The form,
And the meaning of our experience,
Individually,
And examine them thoroughly.
We examine their causes, conditions, other factors,
And the way they arise in dependencies,
In all their variety.
We scrutinize them until
We understand the meaning of what we see
Without visualizing anything
To practice a higher perception.

After we have done something virtuous,
We bind it into one
With all the virtues that it signifies,
And dedicate it toward the unsurpassed enlightenment
Of all sentient beings.

It is said that while we may not,
At this time,
Have gathered together the virtues we must transform,
Our prayer has great significance,
So we will acquire them.
We will succeed in our objective
Because we have made these prayers.
This is why our minds are, themselves,
Most important.

So it is that all our virtues,
Being ornamented by recollection,
Dedication, and holy prayers,
Are not exhausted,
But are augmented,
And become causes toward the magnificent objectives
Of everyone,
Ourselves and other beings.

Advice to Kublai Khan

So these things that we take into our experience,
As well as compounded dharmas in all their variety,
All depend on causes and conditions,
And are not made out of their own essences.

They appear in various ways
To our polluted minds,
Due to our habits.
These experiences are not true.
We contemplate that they are illusions
That have occurred through a variety of conditions,
Or dreams that are mixed into our sleep.

Uncompounded dharmas are nothing but attributions.
The sounds of meaningless words
Are compounded by our conceptualizations.
Those who believe they are meaningful
Are mad.

The dependent origin of relative causes and conditions
Is not a deception.
We will experience the full fruition
Of the things that we do.
We must, therefore, not ignore
The way of causes and conditions.

To want it to be true that things exist
Is a way of seeing things as permanent.

There are no dharmas that do not have a time and place.
When we separate them according to their time and place,
It will be impossible for there to be a solitary entity.
There is no one,
So where will the many come from?
There is also nothing that is other than these.
So saying: "They exist"
Is a miserable idea.

If nothing were long,
How could anything be short?
Existence is not made up out of any essence.
So how could there be a view
In which non-existence is natural?

We make things clear
With these two disparaging observations:
That neither a thing to prove nor a referent exists.
There are no dharmas that both exist and do not exist,
And there are none that are neither.
You must use a clear wisdom to understand this.

If our idea is that
Because the mind has no form,
It has no place,
And therefore it is true that it is solitary,
Then there will be
Both taking in and holding onto a multiplicity of appearances
And oneness,
So our minds will also be multiple.
We will turn out to be liars.
But if they are separate,
What will happen to dharmas and reality?

Where does the appearance of duality come from?
What about nirvana being the exhaustion of delusion?

Our taking things in is not made from any essentiality.
Our holding on also has no essentiality.
Those who claim that there is a true luminous awareness
That is other than these,
That is different from these transformations,
Are totally lying to both themselves and others.

There is no essentiality that is unborn from the primordial.
You must comprehensively understand all dharmas
In their true nature,
Which is entirely free from complications,
Then let yourself be without visualizations,
Like the sky.

We also do not reject the way
Of the emptiness of all dharmas.
We do not cut off the flow
Of dependent and connected origination.
This is a miracle.
When we understand these things

Advice to Kublai Khan

It will be more than amazing.
It will be extremely amazing.

You must understand
That all objects are an interactivity
Of appearance and emptiness,
That our minds are also an interactivity
Of awareness and emptiness,
That our path is an interactivity
Of methods and wisdom,
And you must totally immerse yourself in this
In all things.

Dependent origination is relative,
Totally obfuscated,
Like an illusion.
Its true nature is ultimate,
The holy intent,
Emptiness.
There is no separation between these two.
They are interactive.
You must understand all the Dharmas,
Of cause, path, and fruition.

So it is that these five:
The basis, preliminaries, placing ourselves in equanimity,
The follow-up tasks, and the stamping of all things with a seal
Completely subsume all the Dharmas of virtue.

Each has three parts.
When divided up,
There are fifteen.

One who perseveres at all these ways of the Dharma,
In each of these enumerations of the path of virtue,
Will enjoy all the happiness of high status.

He will brilliantly gather up an oceanic collection
Of the two accumulations of merit and wisdom.
He will join himself to the path of nobles
With a clear samadhi.
He will make his wisdom grow
With meditation and practice.

He will use the ends of the path
To reach the end.

The true nature of the mind
Is to be primordially pure.
Its taste is one with its dominion,
In the pacification of our ideas.
When we understand its natural embodiment:
The wisdom of the dominion of the Dharma,
And a perfect store of renunciation,
As they are,

The Dharmas of samsara
Are brilliantly transformed by the path.
Our bodies transform in station,
Into bodies arrayed with markings and exemplary features.
Our speech transforms in station,
Into a speech that has sixty cadences.
Our minds transform in station,
Into three wisdoms that hold knowledge
Of how things are accounted for.
Our problems are transformed in station,
Into the wonders of the Victorious Ones,
And are an endless father.
This is our embodiment in perfect pleasure.

Our karma transforms in station,
Into the wisdom that gets things done,
And a vast account of good works.
This is our manifest embodiment.

The understanding of these things
Is a perfect store.
It endows us with power.

I beg you, Lord of the People,
To forever and with no disruption
Employ yourself like this.

Through the virtue there is
In summarizing the profound intent
Of the highest vehicle,
And offering it to the people of the Dharma,

Advice to Kublai Khan

May all living beings,
With you being foremost, O King,
Attain the holy status of Buddhahood.

By offering this Excellent Work,
On the life of the Dharma,
The bravery in my mind grows,
O Lord of the People.
So I beg you to contemplate these few solicitations
Right from the start and without delay.

Now is the time for you
To lengthen the lifespan of your body,
To support the glory of your lineage and your descendants,
And to persevere at these methods for finding total freedom.
It is fitting that you persevere at them without delay.

The glory of the Dharma that we teach has not failed,
And we have a Dharma King such as yourself.
This is an opportunity for those who wear saffron.
What do you feel about them in your heart?

I am not old in my age,
But my body's strength has diminished,
And my mind is slack with a casual attitude.
For these reasons,
I am seeking out a secluded place
To pursue the intent of the Dharma.
I beg you to enact your kindness
To accommodate this.

This Excellent Work of Advice for the King was composed by Phagpa in the year of the female iron sheep (1271/72 A.D.), on the eighth day of the month of the rooster, in the land of Shingkun.

Chogyal Phagpa

AN ORNAMENT TO ILLUMINATE THE ORATIONS: A PRESENTATION ON THE EXCELLENT WORK OF ADVICE TO THE KING

rGyal po la gdams pa'i rab tu byed pa'i rnam par bshad pa
gsung rab gsal ba'i rgyan

I bow to all the Buddhas and to all the Bodhisattvas.

I will bow with undivided faith to the omniscient sun,
Blazing with the brilliance
Of a hundred hundred thousand million wonders,
That entirely overcomes
The piles of brambles that are our problems,
And steals the fog of ignorance away from living beings.

Now the Dharma King commands that I make
The shores of the great ocean
Of the Victorious One's orations
Easy to understand.

So I present this,
In keeping with the Victorious One's words,
And my guru's orations,
In reverence to the wishes of the king,
The lord of the people.

Here, I have brought together well the heart-essence of all the brilliantly diffuse orations made by the one who moves in bliss, and I present the ways of bringing it easily into our experience. I will explain this Refined Presentation of Advice for the King as it is found in the orations of this holy guru to the extent of my ability.

Words that speak of worship for our teacher are carefully placed at the beginning, out of a desire to compose a treatise. This is to accord with the practices of holy ones, to bring the work of authoring a treatise to completion, and to bring vast merit to ourselves and those who will come after.

This is the vow to explain:

After bowing to the supreme glory of the Buddha
Glorifying him in words of fame and renown
For his glory in the miraculous intent of his virtues,
I will present this unto the glory of our holy ruler.

Here, the "bowing" is to take up a specific topic. You may ask who he is bowing to. It is the Buddha. You might ask what kind of Buddha it is. He is the most outstanding of the glorious, and is especially noble.

This "glory" is of two sorts:

There is the statement: "Your banner of fame is renowned throughout the three worlds," which shows the glory of words of extensive praise and fame. The Auditors and Private Buddhas do have class in their virtues of reason and liberation, but they do not have extensive renown and fame. Now Brahma, Indra, Vishnu and their kind do have names that are famous and praised, but nothing more. This is why they don't turn out to be especially noble. There are the words "miraculous virtues," so that we can be rid of worries in our thinking.

The glory that is significant, however, is to cut through the obstructions made by emotional and intellectual problems at the root. There is an amazing and miraculous virtue in the knowledge of what is to be known, both as it is and as it is described. This glory is retained exclusively by the Buddha.

The Auditors, Private Buddhas, and Bodhisattvas do not have these, so there is no need to mention the teachers of the world, such as Brahma.

Master Maticitra has said:

The omniscient one has every virtue,

What is more, his virtues do not fail.
He does not harbor a single problem,
Or any tendency that might go with it.

The fact is that those who are the greatest of the great in this world praise and perform services to the Buddha, so the fame of his repute is unlimited.

You might ask just who the person is who is bowing. It is the author of this treatise himself.

If you ask what actions he undertakes after speaking out his homage for this especially noble being, I beg you to listen to this scripture of advice to the potentate. It is a glory for the holy.

Now "potentate" is a word for a king. This is because he exercises power over the kingdom. It is also used to describe common beings, so to show that he is especially noble, he is called "holy," for he maintains the glory of the holy Dharma and upholds holy practices. This also describes a king who protects the Dharma.

He takes a vow to explain, with the statement of worship preceding it, to put a stop to false ideas which might consider that because this king is being cared for by a very pure companion in virtue, and in the past has learned many profound and vast Dharmas from his lips, making him unconfused about the ways of the world and of the Dharma, there is no need to instruct him with this scripture. This is why he uses two verses to present these words about the necessity and connectedness of this treatise. Then he proclaims:

> *Bend down and listen to this exposition*
> *Of the two kinds of classics.*
> *You have seen them in your heart,*
> *And have become engaged in them,*
> *But as it is with the songs of musicians*
> *And the instruments they play,*
> *Why shouldn't poets take them up once again?*

> *The Sage has proclaimed numerous heaps of Dharmas*
> *So that he might help his abundant disciples.*
> *All of them are sources to be taken into our experience,*
> *And nothing more.*
> *So you must know their ways as follows.*

Now of these, the earlier verse is to remove false ideas that we worry about. It says: "Bend down and listen to this exposition of the two kinds of classics, those of the world and those of the Dharma. You have seen them in your heart in the past, and you are already engaged in them, but while we may have already heard lyrics and music, merely for the sake of play and romance, the musicians broadcast them every day. So when poets please us with poetry on the way of the holy Dharma, which is of the utmost importance, why shouldn't we sing them once again? It is right that we sing them."

In his Letter to King Gautamiputra, the noble Nagarjuna proclaimed:

> You have seen this in your heart,
> And have surely taken it in,
> But the dust of stones makes the winter moonlight brighter,
> Doesn't it?

This is an analogous statement.

The latter verse presents real words on necessity and connectedness. The thing that is to be discussed is everything that the innumerable heaps of the Dharma proclaim.

The necessity is to know that the way of the Dharma is so, and to know how to take it into our experience. The need for this necessity is presented with the saying: "The Sage succeeded in helping his abundant disciples, and you too, O King, must succeed." After that he says: "I beg you, O Lord of Men, to practice in this way."

The connectedness was not proclaimed to force him to accept something.

Now a "Sage" here is someone who has extraordinary abilities in his body, speech, and mind. He is a Buddha. He proclaims heaps of Dharmas beyond number to accommodate this abundant disciples' health, wishes, and dormant tendencies.

Now "*chos*" is Dharma. Grammatically, *Dha* is *Dhara*, or holding on, and *Ma* is *Mana*, which is mind, so it means: "Holding the mind." In their obscured reality, all dharmas hold to their own individual characteristics. When we investigate them, however, dharmas have no characteristics of any kind. When we hold the significance of this in our minds we are able to hold onto something other than samsara.

"Heap" is *Skandha*. This is because it is a collection or gathering of letters, names, and words. You might say: "There have been proclaimed to be eighty thousand heaps of the Dharma, haven't there? How could they be beyond counting?"

Eighty thousand was proclaimed when Ananda took an estimate of the Auditors. Who could estimate the heaps of Dharmas that have been proclaimed to accommodate the health, wishes, and dormant tendencies of all his abundant disciples? The King of Samadhi Sutra also proclaims:

> Who could take measure of the Buddha's Dharmas?
> The mind of such a person
> Will be exceptionally crazy.
> We cannot take measure of something
> That transcends measurement.
> The totality of our leader's wonders is inconceivable.

Now none of these immeasurable heaps of Dharma represent the interests of listening, arguing, portents of evil, and so on. They represent the interest of taking what we work to succeed at into our experience, and nothing more. All of them were presented for our assistance and happiness, and nothing else. On this point, Master Maticitra proclaimed:

> You speak to assist,
> And work to assist.
> This is what you teach.
> When I put it in my head it blazes.
> Why would I not practice it?

The Commentary also proclaims:

> Our protector proclaimed the path that he sees.
> He did not proclaim lies,
> For there would be no fruition.
> He put all these compositions together
> For the sake of other beings
> Because his heart has love.
>
> One who has knowledge does not proclaim lies.
> One who has love practices speaking to assist.

Now you may ask: "If that is the case, are the baskets of the Auditors and Private Buddhas also to be taken into a Bodhisattvas experience?"

It is so. The baskets of the Auditors and Private Buddhas were presented primarily as vows against problematic behaviors that are physical and verbal. They do not contradict the trainings of a Bodhisattva. In fact, it is when they are enveloped in an enlightened attitude that we move along the path of the perfect Buddha.

The seven classes of vows for personal freedom
Will always support different vows,
So they are nothing more than an opportunity for us
To engender the vow of a Bodhisattva.

And again:

The community of those who have been ordained
Maintains immeasurable virtues.
For this reason they are superior
To householder Bodhisattvas who are serious in their vows.

The trainings of a Bodhisattva are primarily vows for the problematic behaviors of our minds, and do not contradict the trainings of Auditors and Private Buddhas. The fruitions achieved by Auditors and Private Buddhas do not offer any vast assistance to other beings, those who do not understand the path or the unborn. They do not eliminate our intellectual obstructions, and are not intentionally concerned with them. Their fruition is that we accomplish our own objectives, we understand that the base is unborn, and we eliminate obstructions caused by our emotional problems. These are also things that Bodhisattvas must accomplish.

Furthermore, it is necessary that the paths of Auditors and Private Buddhas be taught. This is so that disciples in the classes of Auditors and Private Buddhas may be trained. If they had been explained just so that we listen to them without practicing them, they would not be meaningful. The Commentary proclaims:

Those who love must overcome sorrow,
So they use methods for a genuine integration.
We may read about the reasons these methods are there,
But they are difficult to describe.

The Victorious One's Mother[26] also proclaims:

Bodhisattvas must know the pathway of the Auditors.

And:

Bodhisattvas must know the pathway of the Private Buddhas.

There are a vast number of such proclamations.

---
[26] rGyal ba'i yum

Furthermore, the Buddhas of the past studied innumerable heaps of the Dharma when they were learning. When they reached their fruition they knew innumerable heaps of Dharmas. So this is also proven through reason.

It is necessary that we take all the heaps of the Dharma into our experience. So you may ask: "What is the way to take them into our experience?"

It says: "You must know this way to include a few ways that are to be discussed below, a few involving settling ourselves into equanimity, and a few ways that involve the stamping of a seal."

This is how the preamble of the treatise is presented, there follows the presentation of the actual treatise, which is primarily about the way to take the instructions of the holy Dharma into our experience. First, it teaches how we must use the way of the basis to take it into our experience:

People in fear and those bound by shame
Do not break the laws made by the king.
Just so, those who live in keeping with the way
Augment their glory without harm,
And are praised, even by the king.

This statement is a teaching by analogy. The analogy is that people who are afraid that they may be executed by the king, or who are bound by shame, worrying about being ridiculed by other people, do not break the laws made by the king, and because they live in the way of the law, they are not harmed by being executed by the king, and their glory, things like their wealth and their hereditary line, will flourish. They will also receive words of praise from the king, why even mention the ministers and their kind?

In order to keep track of beginners who have karma,
The Sage made rules that are common among the vehicles.
We take them up according to our own ability to practice them,
Using rituals complete in their branches,
So that both those who are terrified
By the sorrows of the world,
Visible and invisible,
And the hosts of noble ones who see the other side,
Might work things out in their hearts.

We are bound by shame,
And we guard ourselves in keeping with the way.
This is the basis for happiness in this world,

Both visible and invisible,
And for all the wonders of total freedom.
We become worthy of the offerings of gods and humans,
And we are praised,
Even by the Buddhas.

The Sage is the Buddha. Beginners having karma refers to the classes of Auditors and Private Buddhas. It is proclaimed:

> A massive number of dreadlock Bodhisattvas from the dominion of the world called: "Observed by God" arrived here in this Buddha-field. They observed the mandala of the Blessed One's retinue, and addressed the Blessed One: "There is a serious majority of Auditors and Private Buddhas in the Blessed One's retinue."

The Blessed One gave an oration:

> "Those who abide in your Buddha-field are vigorous Bodhisattvas, every one. In my Buddha-field there are many who are childish or are beginners. This is why the retinue of Auditors is a majority."

Our necessity is to care for those who are Auditors or Private Buddhas.

The rules that are included within the Vinaya basket are common to the vehicles. There are the things we stop doing, the things we practice, and the teachings, and they may be either connected or associated by inference. Essentially, there are the fasting, the novice, the monk, and the rest. They accommodate our own ability to practice them.

Our objects are our ordination master, our Master, and the Sangha, from whom we go for refuge in a ritual. We present our request. Then we must take up the rites, the Rites for the Four,[27] and other such, in full perfection. This is because the correct way to take them on is in the rule of the way that is evident through signs. The Vinaya Sutra also proclaims: "When we are finished with the ritual we must not discontinue the rites." We take them up according to our ability to practice them, but it is proclaimed in the Sutra of the Medicine Guru, the King of Vaidurya Light:

> There are those who keep to five bases of training.
> There are those who keep to ten bases of training.
> There are those who keep to four hundred bases of training.

---
[27] bZhi'i las

Monks who have departed from living in a house
Keep two hundred fifty bases of training.
Nuns keep to five hundred bases of training.

Again, this same source proclaims:

Any sons of heritage or daughters of heritage who truly abide in fasting with its eight branches for one year or three months will maintain their bases of training.

If we take on a big load by practicing something we are not capable of, we will fail, and it will become a cause of suffering. The King of Samadhi proclaims:

Those who corrupt the rule of the way
Go on to be animals.
Their large amount of learning
Will not protect them.

You may ask for the reason. It is out of fear for suffering when we see it, and for unseen suffering in future worlds, such as in the three kinds of horrible lives. The Ornament of the Sutras proclaims:

The eye of the Buddha's direct perception,
His teachings,
Will protect even me.
At this time my wisdom is not obstructed.
It is therefore inappropriate to be equanimous.

Engaging in the Practice proclaims:

The Buddhas and the Bodhisattvas
Have a vision that nothing hinders.
I will forever present myself
Before their visible presence.

The hearts of the noble community that sees the other side will have shame. We bind our sensory doors with shame, and keep the things that we have taken on in the proper way. The fruition of this in visible Dharmas is that we will have a long life in this lifetime, have many enjoyments, and all the rest. In future rebirths that we do not see we will have the happinesses of high status. The Sutras proclaim:

Those who maintain the rule of the way
Would not harm even a poisonous snake,
A large black naga.
Why even talk about other beings?

And again:

For the living who go in goodness,
This is a reliable bridge to cross the waters.

There are a vast number of such proclamations.

Not only do we acquire the happiness of the world,
We use a higher perception to get rid of our emotional problems.
Through getting rid of our emotional problems,
The sorrows of samsara do not come to pass.
Through this we attain total emancipation from every fetter.

That is how it is, but Master Śantideva proclaimed:

A higher perception that brilliantly maintains peaceful abiding
Is a knowledge that thoroughly removes emotional problems.
To start out, we must seek peaceful abiding.
Through it we will have no attachment to the world,
And we will succeed in true purity.

The Three Hundred Verses proclaims:

The decisive rule of the way removes sorrow.
It decimates the demonic roots
That are destructive and acquisitive perspectives.
It overcomes the glorious ones,
And those who use flowers for arrows.

We will also become worthy of the offerings of gods and humans. Master Maticitra proclaimed:

You are an Auditor with no desires,
And hold to dignified things.
It is for these reasons that the gods join their palms,
Make prayers,
And make offerings to you as if you were a great dignitary.

Now receiving the offerings of gods and humans is not all, and this is why our teacher made high praise of the rule of the way, for we will receive the praise of even the Buddha, with words such as these:

> O Monk Who Holds to the Rule of the Way,
> You bear light.
> You are famous as a keeper of the rule of the way.
> You have achieved happiness.

In this way, he taught the necessity of teaching the trainings that are found in the Auditor's baskets, a teaching that is primarily about our physical and verbal practices, then he taught the necessity of teachings for Bodhisattvas, which are mental practices that are primarily for the sake of other beings.

> These three worlds are nothing but sorrow.
> Nirvana is also nothing but peace.
> So we look at samsara and nirvana
> As objects of compassion.
> And pray for them.

This verse presents our first reason for developing an enlightened attitude. Lord Maitreya proclaimed:

> The five kinds of living things have no happiness.
> There is no sweet smell in a latrine.

In this way, the realm of desire is where we are actually involved in desire and we live with both the causes and results of sorrow. The realm of form is where we are not actually involved in desire, but live with the causes of sorrow. The formless realm is where there is nothing but sorrow. Master Maticitra proclaimed:

> People who are not directed toward your Dharma
> Are blinded by ignorance.
> Even if they go to the pinnacle of the world,
> They accomplish only the world,
> Where sorrow is constantly occurring.

If this is so, you may ask, do we not feel happiness and equanimity?

Even though there are situations where we have happiness, there will be a time when we lose it. This is because there are sorrows that we will come to experience. Furthermore, all compounded things are pervaded by impermanence. This pervasion encompasses the sorrow of compounded things, but this is not obvious to ordinary individuals. It is said:

> The sorrow of compounded things is like a hair.
> The childish are like the palm of a hand.
> Noble people are like eyes.
> This is why the childish don't see.

So you may ask: "The absence of sorrow is something that the Auditors and Private Buddhas have, so shouldn't we practice these paths?"

Their nirvana is merely the pacification of gross sufferings. We do not get rid of the natural embodiment of our mind, or its cause: Our habitual tendencies through ignorance. We do not reach the level of great happiness, which is the abode of the Mahayana's compassion. The Sutra of the Lion's Roar of Śrīmala proclaims:

> Blessed One, this is in agreement with the analogy that describes the three worlds coming about through karmic causes that are defiled through holding to conditions that we have taken on. Blessed One, the three bodies, whose nature is the mind, of Arhats, Private Buddhas, and Bodhisattvas that have attained empowerment, occur through karmic causes that are not defiled through holding to conditions, the level of the habitual tendencies of our ignorance. Blessed One, the habitual tendencies of our ignorance manifest as these three bodies, whose nature is the mind, on these three levels. These are the conditions under which inexhaustible karma is actually formed.

There are a vast number of such proclamations.

Lord Maitreya has proclaimed:

> Renunciates who develop an attitude that is worthy of greatness
> Will consider helping others,
> And finding the means for this.
> They will perceive the significance of a great inspiration
> And the highest reality.
> They will renounce their happiness,
> And go on to peace.

Here, "peace" means that they are no longer concerned with those things, and that they meditate on compassion. Maitreya proclaimed:

Those who are seized by compassion
Have love.
Their minds are not fixed,
Even on peace.
There is no need to speak of the happiness of this world,
Or attachment to their own lives.

And again:

The Tathagata took his seat there,
And while he sat on the high peak of the mighty mountain,
He looked at the living beings.
In his heart there was love
For the living beings who truly delight in peace.
Why mention the other ones who truly delight in the world?

For these reasons, we may get rid of samsara, where there is no happiness and there is suffering, as well as the rough sorrows, and we may pray for the peace of nirvana, which is not an acquisition of some level of great happiness, but in either case we must see that all of them are objects for our compassion.
This shows the second reason to develop an enlightened attitude.

The Buddha is the only one
Who has no sorrow and removes every sorrow,
Who has found great happiness
And seeks out happiness for everyone.
What is more,
He was someone like me.
His methods made him able to succeed.
That is why I too must certainly attain Buddhahood.

This is what is called: "Expressing an intent."

"The Buddha is the only one that has no personal suffering and removes the sorrows of others, that has found the status of great personal happiness and seeks everywhere the highest happiness for other beings, so I too must certainly attain the same kind of Buddhahood." This is how we must express our intent. This oration was presented so that we might use it for taking an oath in the presence of our intended object.

Now you may think that there is indeed a great necessity that we attain Buddhahood, but that people like us won't be able to succeed in this.

The Buddha, however, was someone like us. He took a methodical pathway into his experience and was able to succeed in perfecting his stores of renunciation and understanding.

You may say that it will not happen that we achieve a perfect store of renunciation, for filth is the nature of our minds and we will not be able to get rid of it. Even if we could get rid of it, we would not know the methods for doing this, and just like filth from our bodies, we get rid of it, but it comes back again.

This is not so. This is because the nature of the mind is clear light. It is because we get rid of its cause. It is because even though we do not know the cause of this filth we get rid of it by immersing ourselves in its remedy, which is wisdom. The Commentary proclaims:

> It will be exhausted because it has a cause,
> And we immerse ourselves in its remedy.
> We use a knowledge of the nature of its cause
> To succeed in this understanding.

We will be able to build up a perfect store of understanding. Immersion into emptiness is not a Dharma for the mind. When we are immersed in it, it becomes infinite. The Treasure of Logical Reason[28] proclaims:

> Through a good study of methods and wisdom
> Causes and conditions become each other,
> And we achieve a vision of wisdom:
> How things are and how they are accounted for.

So it is that we must develop an enlightened attitude with considerations for these two causes: A heart's love for sentient beings, and a desire for Buddhahood.

This is how I describe developing an enlightened attitude by way of a practice of cutting through things thoroughly, and then teach it by way of ceasing this cutting. It has been proclaimed:

> We must meditate on the highest enlightened attitude
> Without apprehension,
> Without a casual attitude,
> And without deceit.

---

[28] Tshad ma rigs pa'i gter

Apprehension is the thought that even if we can, when we exert ourselves, achieve a mere escape, we will not be able to succeed at Buddhahood. This is because we will have to gather up accumulations of merit and wisdom for a duration of three immeasurable eons, because we will have to work to help innumerable sentient beings, we will have to know infinite things that must be known, and that each word of the Dharma turns out to be three thousand tongues of fire, so we will not be able to engage in the difficulties of crossing over them.

We turn away from these ideas. Engaging in the Practice proclaims:

If sentient beings were people,
We would not take these apprehensions seriously,
For even though they are inestimable,
They are attaining perfect enlightenment
Every second.

Master Candragomin proclaimed:

Being thrown into the interconnectedness of samsara
Is like being thrown into space.
We do not understand this
Because we are being born, dead, or in transition.
When we throw it off,
And liberate a single soul from it,
There is nothing to be ashamed of.

There is a necessity that we work to help innumerable sentient beings, so our accumulations will quickly come together. This is because when we work to help infinite sentient beings, we will also get infinite roots of virtue. Master Śantideva also spoke on this:

The power of an enlightened attitude
Brings our previous evils to an end,
And acts as a cause for an ocean of merit.
The groups of Auditors say that it is the best.

We do amass accumulations over a period of three immeasurable eons, but this is not a long time for Bodhisattvas who are cleansing their minds for the sake of sentient beings. The teachings of the Licchavi Renowned for Filthlessness proclaim that for Bodhisattvas who are training in condensed samsara, an eon starts to seem like seven days. For Bodhisattvas who are training in expanded samsara, seven days starts to seem like an eon.

Furthermore, once we are on the great path of accumulation we play on four magical feet. Once we are on the path of applications we do not fall into a horrible life. Once we are on the path of seeing we will not go back to being ordinary individuals. In such ways we gradually enjoy numerous benefits, and we come to dwell on pathways that have no sorrow. So what is wrong with it taking a long time? Master Śantideva also proclaimed:

> So once we have mounted the horse of an enlightened attitude,
> Which protects us and clears everything away,
> We move from happiness on to happiness.
> So who would have a casual attitude about knowing the mind?

When we look at the Buddha fields in the ten directions with eyes that are entirely pure, there are an inconceivable number of Bodhisattvas who are starting to develop their attitudes and engage in their practices. Among them, why should I be the only one who is inferior? Engaging in the Practice proclaims:

> When those who are bees, flies, wasps, or even worms
> Develop the strength of perseverance
> They will attain unexcelled enlightenment,
> Which is difficult to attain.

When it says: "To practice hardships for the sake of the Dharma, to distribute even such gifts as one's head or limbs, to support a companion. . ." these are practices which are to be acquired. To give a mouthful of food in a situation where we have not yet achieved a level is a small effort. If we had not acquired a body, through time without beginning, there would be no cause for our enlightenment. This body is the only thing that is sure to be a cause for our enlightenment. This is proclaimed so that we may understand and have the thought: "I have found the best thing that can be found!"
The Noble Eight Thousand Lines proclaims:

> I will not give up on these sentient beings. I must liberate all these sentient beings from heaps of sorrow that have no counting. A hundred of my bodies may be chopped up, but at the least I will not develop thoughts of doing harm.

Bodhisattvas must develop their attitudes with thoughts like these. When we live with an attitude like this we do not practice conceptions that we are doing anything difficult, for we do not live with the attitude that we are doing difficult things. Master Śantideva proclaimed:

> The giving away of things like vegetables
> Must be practiced at the beginning,
> For guidance.
> Once we are accustomed to this,
> We will progressively give up even our own flesh.
>
> What difficulties will those who begin to think
> That their own bodies resemble vegetables and such things
> Have
> In giving away their flesh and such things?

A casual attitude comes to our minds through bad friends, the experience of suffering, and other such causes, which become obstructions to our practice of the path. Śantideva proclaimed:

> If fishers, farmers, and those in the class of fishermen,
> Who care only for their own lives,
> Tolerate the damage caused by heat, cold, and such things,
> Why shouldn't someone like me tolerate them,
> For the sake of the happiness of living beings?

This is a way to eliminate a casual attitude so that we will use the Dharmas for the world and for peace that are taught above to be stable, and not be deceived. The Ornament of Sutras proclaims:

> We are stable.
> We are not deceived by bad friends, sorrow,
> Or listening to profundities.

Enlightenment is the exhaustion of filth, from the primordial, and is a wisdom that understands how it is with the unborn. Maitreya proclaimed:

> The exhaustion of filth
> And the wisdom of the unborn
> Is called: "Enlightenment."

An enlightened attitude is described in the Buddha Avatamsaka Sutra:

It is difficult to pray for enlightenment.
Why mention to promise it?

So there are two parts to this. I have heard from the lips of the Dharma Lord that the thought in our minds that says: "I must attain enlightenment" is a prayerful attitude. When we take a vow in the presence of our intended object, this is the generation of a prayerful attitude. The thought in our minds that says: "I am engaging in the practice of enlightenment" is an engaged attitude. When we take a vow in the presence of our intended object, this is the generation of an engaged attitude.

The essence is a desire to attain enlightenment for the sake of others. Maitreya proclaimed:

The generation of an attitude
Is done for the sake of others.
It is a desire for fully perfected enlightenment.

Now this kind of enlightened attitude is superior to the enlightenments of the Auditors and Private Buddhas, so it has been proclaimed to be supreme.

Here I would add: "You, O Lord of the Earth, have not developed this, so you must meditate on what it means to develop it."

So once it has been explained that we must take an enlightened attitude into our experience as it is found in the Baskets for Bodhisattvas, it then presents the requirement that we take the samaya into our experience as it is found in the Baskets for Vision Keepers. This is what it says:

When we transgress them we will burn in hell.
There is happiness in keeping them.
We will immediately attain a miraculous fruition of happiness.
Once we have taken on samaya,
We must guard them as dearly as our lives.

When we take them, we say: "After I take on these samaya I will keep them."

The Tibetan word *Dam tshig* is samaya.

Regarding the time during which we engage in them, we must not break them from the very moment that we acquire them.

If you ask who we take them from, the Fifty Verses on the Guru proclaims:

He is stable, subdued, and has intelligence.
He has patience, is honest, and is not deceitful.
He knows the applications for mantras and Tantras.
He is most expert in these ten realities.
He is skilled in the work of drawing out mandalas.
He is most peaceful,
And his senses are subdued.

We take them from a guru who has these ten defining qualities.

You may ask in what manner we guard them. We guard them as dearly as our own lives. The reason that we must guard them as dearly as our lives was proclaimed by Aryadeva:

A king who is capable of cutting off our heads
Is also capable of granting us a kingdom.

According to this method, when we break them we will be reborn into one of the three kinds of horrible lives, which include hell, but if we keep them we will immediately attain the living conditions of one of the Eight Lords or a similar life, and ultimately we will attain an amazing and miraculous fruition of happiness. "Immediately" means that we will attain our fruition in this lifetime, during the bardo, or in not more than sixteen lifetimes. This is therefore superior in specific ways to the vehicles of the Perfections.

We need six months to bring a harvest to maturity, but when we use special mantras and substances, we bring it to maturity in one day. Just so, we need to gather our accumulations for three immeasurable eons to reach success at Buddhahood, but when we connect with specialized methods we will succeed in getting a result in this very lifetime, or sometime soon. The Careful Division of the Three Vows speaks on this:

In the same way that those who work
According to the ways of business
Gradually mature their harvest,
Those who enter the path of the Perfections
Take three immeasurables to become perfect Buddhas.

A seed that has been planted with mantras
Takes one day to mature a harvest.
Just so, when we know the methods of the Vajrayana
We succeed at Buddhahood in this very life.

This brings things together at the conclusion to teach them.

Then I proclaim:

So it is that there are three vows for the three vehicles.
They are the basis for the development, maintenance, and prosperity
Of all our wondrous virtues,
And those of others.
I recommend that we depend on them
At the very beginning.

This follows the methods described above. The three vows for the three vehicles, the Arhat, Bodhisattva, and Secret Mantra, are taken up right at the beginning, when we enter the teachings, and are recommended in the teachings.
You may ask what need we have for them.
At the beginning, they are the basis of developing everything that is wondrous in the world and that transcends the world, for both ourselves and for other beings. In the interim, they are the basis for our continuation. At the end, they are the basis for our flourishing. The Sutra on Maintaining the Rule of the Way Correctly[29] speaks on this:

As if it were a fine vessel,
A vase of jewels,
The rule of the way is the basis of everything.

The King of Samadhi also proclaims:

The meditation on this empty king of samadhi
Sits at the head of the rule of the way.
We constantly place ourselves in a natural equanimity
Regarding all the dharmas.
The classes of childish people will not understand this,
Even though they persevere.

The Tantra that is called: "The Vajra Peak" also proclaims:

Maintenance of the three vows
Is described as our first cleansing.

The noble Nagarjuna also proclaimed:

---
[29] Tshul khrims yang dag par ldan pa'i mdo

The rule is like the earth,
Whether moving or unmoving.
It is the basis and support for every good thing.
You must know this.

So once I have explained taking this into our experience using the way of the basis, I begin to teach three ways to take it into our experience using the way of preparations:

We must ascertain the specifics of the Dharma
Through the Dharma,
For its words are entirely filthless.
It is thoroughly ascertained through two kinds of validation.
It is not contradictory,
And it is virtuous at the beginning, in the middle, and at the end.

Its speaker has unhindered genius.
He does not covet his books,
But teaches them.
He has love.
He removes the problems there are in positions that disagree.
He knows about the acquisition of great power.
He is a Buddha.

This is then linked up with what will be explained in the following, that we must meditate on faith.
You may ask what we are to have faith in. It is the Three Jewels and our guru. The Nirvana Sutra proclaims:

People who are afraid and terrified
Mostly go for refuge to the mountains,
To the forests,
To places of worship in fenced parks,
And to trees.
These refuges are not the best.
These refuges are not worthy of worship.
When we rely on them for support
They are unable to free us from all our sufferings.
The Buddha, Dharma, and Sangha
Are refuges for those who want to be free.
They are the best refuges.
These refuges are worthy of worship.

When we rely on them for support
They liberate us from the great river of sorrow.

Master Śāntipa proclaimed:

Lack of faith is our primary enemy.
Excessive faith is an abode for extreme deviance.
This is why omniscience is a validation.
We will not become omniscient through faith.

We must meditate on a stable faith by way of knowing the virtues of our intended object, and never let ourselves be cut off from it due to extraneous circumstances. The Ornament of the Sutras proclaims:

We know its virtues and our minds do not part from it.
Our samadhi is quick and we savor the fruits.
So we must believe in our teacher.
The children of the Victorious One
Wish for a correctly and completely matured enlightenment.

You may ask: "Through what sorts of methods do we come to understand these virtues?"

We will reach certainty on the specifics of the Dharma through the Dharma. Moreover, the Buddha was the teacher that brought it forth. So we look into the excellent orations that he proclaimed, the same way that we look at the message in a letter to understand its sender.

So you may say: "So once you have proven he is a teacher, using indicators of his results, how will you prove that he is especially superior to other teachers?"

These words are evidenced:

Monks or scholars will do a careful investigation of my orations,
And will take them up
As if they were burning, cutting, and polishing gold,
And not on account of faith.

We will have proof when we look into the specifics of these words. To prove that he possesses knowledge:

The words of the speaker
Are free from pollutants like chit-chat.
The things he speaks on are presented
In any form that may be appropriate.

Such statements as this one make us realize what we have to take measure of, are not in contradiction to a validation by direct perception, and are proven with it. When he says such things as: "All composite things are impermanent," the thing to take measure of is hidden from us, but there is no contradiction in using inferential validation, so we use it in making proofs.

This is the sort of Dharma that exterminates our emotional problems when we hear it, right at the beginning, so it is virtuous. During the interim, when we contemplate it, it smashes the heads of our emotional problems, so it is virtuous. In the end, when we meditate on it, it removes our emotional problems from our presence, so it is virtuous.

Master Maticitra has spoken on this:

To begin at the start,
Your orations steal the minds of those who listen.
They then contemplate them in their minds,
And their lust and stupidity are removed.

And again:

Your proclamations are virtuous in the beginning,
In the middle,
And at the end.
They turn into an ambrosia
For our study, contemplation, meditation, and practice.

When I say:

It is also by this that we recognize the Jewel of the Dharma.
It is virtuous at the beginning, middle, and end.

I am talking about the Dharma of the path of cessation. The remaining half line and the next three lines are on the recognition of the Dharma that is spoken. It says in them:

The Buddha is the one who knows everything
There is to be known.
His speaking is stainless.
The things he speaks have been ascertained through validations.
So it is that he proclaims a Dharma of virtue
Throughout the three times.

This establishes that he is a teacher who has knowledge. The Dharma Lord has proclaimed from his lips:

> The one who sees everything that there is to know
> Is my teacher.

But while he does have knowledge, it will not be sure that he will teach things as he knows them if he does not have love. In that case, the teaching will not happen. So it is that a teacher for those who have love is a teacher that has no covetousness for his books on the vast and profound Dharma, but accommodates it to our thinking. So it is that he is one that has great compassion. Tobtsun Drubje[30] also spoke on this:

> O Guide,
> Through your compassion
> You proclaim the holy Dharma even to fishermen.
> You have said that if it is a fit receiver of the correct explanations
> Evan a dog must be brought to maturity.

The Dharma Lord also proclaimed:

> To the one who looks on the living beings in samsara
> I respectfully bow down.

Now he may have these kinds of knowledge and love, but he may not have great power, and will be oppressed by disagreeable conditions, so we must be sure that he has great power in overcoming evil views. On this point, Lord Maitreya proclaimed:

> It is uncompounded and spontaneously formed.
> It is not to be understood through conditions other than these.
> It has knowledge, love, and power,
> So Buddhahood maintains its two objectives.

There are not more than three mentioned here, but just these three will not suffice for the objective of helping others, his disciples, but by demonstrating that he has these three we establish that he has the strength to reach his own objectives. It is pleasant to explain things this way.

I explain our objects of faith, the Buddha Jewel and the Dharma Jewel, together, then give an explanation of the Sangha Jewel. I say:

---

[30] Thob btsun grub rje

They follow his trail.
Their virtue is a concordant cause for what they are.
They are the finest community.
They share their practice fields.
We ascertain that their field is holy,
For they gather in virtue.

The specifics on a full acceptance of the Sangha were discussed by Master Asanga:

The unsurpassed Tathagata has achieved the full moon,
And engages in a path that goes along with it.

According to this, we do not become followers of beings like Brahma or Iśvara, for we have become followers of our teacher, the completely perfect Buddha.

On the specifics of the virtues there are in this, Maitreya has proclaimed:

The way of the Bodhisattva
Is to become a Tathagata later on,
And to properly liberate sentient beings.
In the world they are equal.

The noble Nagarjuna also said:

The inconceivable Dharmas of the Buddha
Are full with ten powers,
And satiate us with fearlessness.
If we do not complicate them
We will not fail.

The virtues of the Buddha accommodate such things as powers and fearlessness.

When it says: "This is also called an accommodating cause," the cause is our heritage. The word for heritage is *Gotra*. The *o* in *Go* is an *a* and a *u*. The *a* disappears. We put a *ga* with the *u*, and put in a *ṇa* as its condition, to get *guṇa*, which is a virtue. *Tra* is *trāra*, which means liberation.

So based on the on the virtues of the path, our heritage, which is to be liberated from samsara, is accommodated. This is what is explained here, but there is no contradiction.

The ones who maintain these kinds of virtues are not alone. They are a community or an assembly.

When it says: "Supreme," this means that they are superior to ordinary individuals and to the Sangha of Auditors. Lord Maitreya has proclaimed:

> However many there may be,
> Their vision of inner wisdom is pure.
> The community of intelligent ones who do not turn back
> Maintain virtues that are unsurpassed.

This assembly is also the holy ones who are our friends on account of our having a common field of practice.

When it says: "It is because they are planters of seeds in fertile fields that the Sangha Jewel has been proclaimed to be supreme," it means that we can be sure that theirs is the holiest of fields, and that we must believe in them without being divisive.

Once we have recognized that the object for our faith is the Three Jewels, we are taught that we must perfume our gurus. It proclaims:

> *They teach us truly,*
> *Bring boundaries together,*
> *Have the accoutrements of three kinds of virtue,*
> *And kindly contemplate protecting us.*
> *We must be constantly stable in our meditation*
> *On a non-divisive faith in our gurus.*

Working from where it says: "We must meditate on faith," you may ask: "What is our intended object?" It is our guru.

The time period is forever.

The way is that we use the power of our understanding of his virtues to be stable and not be divisive.

You may ask: "What are his virtues?" He truly does teach about the Three Jewels. He teaches that the Buddha is our teacher. The Dharma is our path. The Sangha is our friends. Moreover, he is the one that teaches us the path that lets us attain Buddhahood, and when we practice in keeping with what he teaches, we achieve Buddhahood. He is truly a teacher of Buddhahood.

It is because the things that he talks about develop the path of cessation in our spirits, and that he is capable of teaching the Excellent Orations in his speaking that he is a true teacher of the Dharma. He gets us onto the pathway of the Mahayana and we do not turn back.

The disciples who practice along that path are the holiest of friends, and he truly teaches them to be our Sangha.

As for bringing boundaries together, we are tortured by sorrow and its causes, so we support the Three Jewels that are able to protect us, in the same way that some people who have little power turn to those with fierce voices. The virtues of the three different Jewels have alignments. Our heart's inspiration aligns with the Buddha. Our pure speech aligns with the Dharma. Our bodies align with the Sangha.
Now the Buddha helps us only through his lineage, while our guru helps us directly. He uses a higher recollection to protect us.

So you, O Ruler of the Land, should consider this in your heart, and meditate on faith in your guru.
This technique is described in detail in the Buddha Avatamsaka:

The boy Glorious Appearance and the girl Glorious Intellect spoke:

We must develop the consciousness
That we are the patients.
We must develop the consciousness
That our companion in virtue is a doctor.
We must develop the consciousness
That the Dharma is medicine.
We must develop the consciousness
That a true practice of the Dharma
Is a genuine use of this medicine.

These are some of the things proclaimed there.

After showing that we must have faith in these finest of principles, I teach that we must meditate on compassion for those who have lesser principles:

For those whose true nature it is
To hold to the stream of the cause and the essence,
Just as we wish to be free ourselves from sorrow and its cause,
So does every living being without exception want to be free.
We meditate on great compassion for them,
So they are not stolen.

When we practice non-virtue we live among causes of suffering. Birth, old age, sickness, and death are the essence or nature of our sorrow, and they are not merely occasional events. Their nature is to hold to us continually, and we see that our spirits are miserable. We feel a wishful desire to be free from this. We must know that all sentient beings, none excepted, are also suffering, and we desire to liberate them from this suffering. We do not regret living in samsara.

We and other beings are the same in wanting to be happy and free of sorrow. We must meditate on great compassion so that they will not be stolen away by disagreeable elements, such as the sorrows of samsara. The Sutras proclaim:

> We maintain an attitude that we are equal to others.
> When we discover that others have more sorrow than we do
> We know that the welfare of others prevails over our own.
> Things that are for our own welfare
> Are also for the welfare of others.
>
> So it is that a compassionate being
> Will endure intolerable torments of sorrow on himself.
> He will not use the karma of being tormented in the world
> As an excuse to engage in no great love.

The Sutra of the Questions of Ocean of Intellect proclaims:

> Ocean of Intellect, why is it that while they are entirely liberated from all their obligations, they take birth in the world? This is the great compassion of the Bodhisattvas. They are skilled in methods and are enveloped in wisdom, so they are not bothered by constant emotional problems. In an effort to liberate all of us from the fetters of emotional problems, they also teach the Dharma to sentient beings.

The Sutra on the Correct Compilation of the Dharma proclaims:

> Blessed One, Bodhisattvas must not train in too many Dharmas. Blessed One, Bodhisattvas must take in one Dharma and brilliantly understand it, and all the Blessed One's Dharmas are on the palm of their hands.

You may ask: "What is this one Dharma?" Look here: it is great compassion. Blessed One, through great compassion all the Buddhas' Dharmas are on the palms of the Bodhisattvas' hands.

And again it proclaims:

Blessed One, look here: If, for example, we have control over the force of life, we will also have it over other forces. In the same way, if we have great compassion we will also have the other Dharmas that work towards enlightenment.

The visualization for great compassion is a visualization of sentient beings, and a desire to remove them from their sorrows. If we divide it up, there are three kinds: Visualization of persons, visualization of dharmas, and being without a visualization.

The compassion of Auditors and Private Buddhas is not connected to any applications, so they are unable to work a great vastness of aid for sentient beings. The compassion of Bodhisattvas is connected with applications, so they are able to actually bring aid to sentient beings.

The Ocean of Intellect Sutra proclaims:

Ocean of Intellect, if, for example, the only child of a businessman or home-owner, a child that is loved, adored, needy, and attractive, there being nothing disagreeable in the sight of him, and this lad, being a child, fell into the pit of a latrine while he was dancing, then the mother of the lad and his relatives would see that he had fallen into the pit of a latrine, and on seeing this would let out a great cry. They would be miserable, and let out words of wailing, but they would not enter the pit of the latrine to get the lad out. Then this lad's father would arrive at the place, and see that his only child had fallen into the pit of a latrine, and once he had seen this would hurry up in a speedy way, acting with a desire to get his only son out. Without being nauseated, he would go into the pit of the latrine and get his only son out.

Ocean of Intellect, I have set this example so that you will understand the significance of how this is. You may ask: "How should we look at what this means?"

Ocean of Intellect, the thing that is called: "The pit of a latrine," is a synonym for the three realms. The so-called "only child" is a synonym for sentient beings. Bodhisattvas live with a consciousness that all sentient beings are their only child. The so-called "mother and relatives" are those who become miserable and cry out lamentations when they see that sentient beings have fallen into samsara, but they cannot get them out. They are synonymous with people on the vehicles of Auditors and Private Buddhas. The so-called businessman or home owner is someone who is clean. He is filthless. He has an attitude that is without filth. He is someone who takes rebirth into the three realms in keeping with his wish to make sentient beings who directly understand reality mature. This is a synonym for a Bodhisattva.

I explained compassion previously, with regard to the situation of generating an enlightened attitude. Here again I am explaining compassion, as I am showing how we need compassion for every circumstance on the path. The Ornament of Sutras proclaims:

> From common roots at the first
> There comes a supreme fruition.
> This is the magnificent tree of compassion.

The Master Candrakirti proclaimed:

> It is because love itself
> Is the perfect store of the Victorious One's harvest,
> And we dwell there in pleasure for a long time,
> Like seeds and the water to make them grow,
> Until we understand that they have matured,
> That I begin with a praise of compassion.

So I present faith in a supreme object and the need to meditate on compassion for the lowly. There is evidenced in the Sutra of Inexhaustible Intellect:

> Any Dharma that we come to have faith in
> Through our sense of belief
> Is to be practiced with a sense of perseverance.

This teaches that we meditate on persevering for what we love.

> *We recollect the benefits there are*
> *In the virtues of caring for supreme enlightenment,*
> *For the welfare of others,*
> *And for our temporary objectives,*
> *And we practice them.*
> *We apply ourselves to this everywhere*
> *With a fierce resolve.*

Supreme enlightenment has been proclaimed to be the magnificent enlightenment of our three embodiments. Its virtue is that it is operative in these three embodiments and their good works.
The Ornament of the Sutras proclaims:

> Our own virtue is to delight in and ponder
> Bringing aid to sentient beings.
> We manifest this by being born and performing miracles.
> Our ornaments and practices are a consummate joy.
> Those who are lacking the spirit of compassion
> Will not find it elsewhere.

This and what follows discuss the welfare of others.

The Rosary of Jewels proclaims:

> Through generosity we get an endowment of pleasure.
> Through the rule we get happiness.
> Through patience we get a fine body.
> Through perseverance we shine.
> Through meditation we get peace.
> Through our minds we get liberation.
> Through the love in our hearts,
> We succeed in all things.

When we recollect the benefits there are in virtues that prioritize our temporary conditions, we have a fierce longing to achieve them, and apply ourselves in all things toward these virtues.

Having taught this in detail, what follows is a summary:

So it is that faith, compassion, and a longing attitude
Are preliminaries for all our works.
We use even the slightest element of virtue
To be motivated and to practice.

Just as I have presented in the above, faith, compassion, and a longing attitude are the preliminaries for every act of virtue.

On the topic of faith as a preliminary, the Buddha Avatamsaka proclaims:

Faith is like a leader.
We generate faith as if it was our guide.
It protects all our virtues,
And makes them grow.

Master Nagarjuna also proclaimed:

Our leader to this is wisdom.
Faith leads us to prepare for it.

Compassion is also a preliminary. The Sutra of Inexhaustible Intellect proclaims:

Revered Śāriputra, see here:
The analogy is
That just as exhaling and inhaling the breath
Are preliminaries for our sense of life,
Great compassion is a preliminary
For a Bodhisattva's practice of the Great Vehicle.

Master Śantideva also proclaimed:

We must set compassion before us
Then strive to augment our virtues.

Longing is also a preliminary. The Jewel Construction proclaims:

It resembles a condition for every Dharma.
We are consecrated in the roots of our longing.

Lord Maitreya's Ornament of the Sutras proclaims:

We go where we wish.

At the beginning of the Thirty Two Verses on Generating an Enlightened Attitude it proclaims that through our longings we generate an enlightened attitude.

For this reason, any trifling substance of virtue that comes from generosity or the other virtues will have been achieved through our being motivated by these three.

I have explained how we take this into our experience using the ways of preliminaries. The actual practice was described by the noble Nagarjuna:

Advice to Kublai Khan

The physical embodiments of the Buddhas
Are born in their collections of merit.

It is proclaimed that we must use visualizations in our meditations, so that we may achieve this physical body.

We look at bodies that are before us,
Or our own,
As being embodiments of the physique of the lord of sages.
Our place is a Buddha Field.
Everyone who is born and is alive
We make out to be a Buddha,
A child of the Buddha,
Or a student.
We use an ocean of gift-clouds
To make offerings to ourselves and others
Of all the pleasures that are the objects our five senses.

We may start from where it says: "We must look at and meditate." As for how we are to meditate, there are two sorts: we meditate on what is before us or else we meditate on our own bodies.

What should we meditate on? The physical body of the lord of sages. Common sages are said to be Auditors or Private Buddhas. In an effort to show that he is not common, it says: "Lord." He has been empowered into the ten empowerments of life, karma, and all the rest. He resembles the foremost or the lord of the mandala of Auditors, Private Buddhas, and Bodhisattvas that are his retinue.

He is embodied in two ways: The Dharma body and the physical body. The Dharma body is not to be looked at or seen by others. The Uttaratantra proclaims:

This is like the sun rising in the sky where we see clouds.
None of the intelligent or the noble ones,
Who have the eye of intelligence,
See you in one place.

Blessed One,
Your Dharma body has endless intelligence,
And sees everything that may be known
Throughout the dominion of the endless sky.

So we must look at the physical body.

The King of Samadhi proclaims:

Your bodies resemble the hue of gold.
You are much more beautiful
Than the lords of the world.
Bodhisattvas who engage their minds in this visualization
Are settled into equanimity.

If we describe this approach as it appears in the Jewel Construction, the Buddhas of the present blaze with their markings and exemplary features like the color of gold. They beam out inestimable light and light rays. At first we meditate on one. Then we build from that until we meditate that there are a great many of them. We meditate from one up to seven days, then from seven on up to a great many days. We will have a clear vision of the Buddhas of the present, and we will have visions of them teaching the Dharma and other good things. When we have these kinds of clear visions, we must investigate where these Buddhas come from, where they dwell, and where they depart to. On such investigation, we will understand that they do not come from anywhere. They do not dwell anywhere. They do not depart for anywhere. Through understanding these things, we will also understand that all dharmas are just the same.

The King of Samadhi also proclaims:

When our conceptions about definitions
Are fully terminated,
We will dwell in an undefined state,
And we will fully understand
The emptiness of all dharmas.

Those who dwell on the Dharma body
Will understand that all material things lack substance.
They will terminate their conceptions about material things.
So they will not look at the physical body
Of the lord of sages.

You have been instructed,
So you must take this in.
This is how those who have ideas
About a multitude of impurities
Use their ideas while they dwell in them
To let their minds flow with the way things are.

We also do not meditate on only our teacher.
The place we live is a Buddha field,
Formed from a foundation
Of a multitude of precious jewels.
It is smooth like the palms of our hands.
If we push down on it, it sinks.
If we jump on it, it makes us fly.
This is how we look at it.

We meditate that everyone who is born and lives
Is a child of the Victorious One,
Or a student.

The chapter on Entirely Pure Concerns for Practice in the Buddha Avatamsaka speaks on these things in detail:

When we see people adorned with jewelry,
We must see them as Bodhisattvas ornamented with virtues.
If we see them without jewelry,
We must see them as not being ornamented by virtues.

These are among the things proclaimed there.

The Victorious One is the Buddha. It is because he overcomes every unacceptable position that must be removed that he is like a king that is victorious in a war. He is also victorious because he has achieved inconceivable stores of wisdom, which is a cure. It is as if he had received the larger part when wealth was distributed.

His children are the Bodhisattvas. It has been explained that they are like the sons of kings due to their ability to retain the lineage of the Buddha.

His students are Auditors. This is because they listen to him and want to learn, yet even when they have finished their learning, they have no special methods, and are unable to retain the lineage of the Buddha. They have been described as resembling the daughters of kings.

Lord of the People, you must use such considerations as these to take all your experiences of attractive forms, sounds, smells, and tastes, the pleasant things that come to your five senses, and those of others, into an ocean of gift-clouds, as if they had been brought forth by the magical manifestations of the All Good One, and in consideration that you yourself and others are the Victorious One and his children, you must make offerings.

Likewise, we do not meditate on and make offerings to the Buddhas alone. We are taught that we should also meditate on and make offerings to our companions in virtue, taking them as a group.

Once we are aware that our guru and all the Victorious Ones,
Without exception,
Are essentially the same in their form and good works,
And that there is no duality,
We contemplate at all times that they are before us,
Are at the crown of our heads,
Or they sit in the center of the lily of our hearts,
And we present them our requests,
Or we meditate that there is no duality.

A guru is described in the above. When it says: "Supreme," it means that he has certain characteristics. These characteristics were described by lord Maitreya:

Serve a companion in virtue who is subdued,
Peaceful, and most calm,
One who encourages us to persevere in virtue,
Rich with the higher transmissions,
One who has a brilliant understanding of reality,
And is skilled in speaking,
One who is a loving person,
And has given up his regrets.

As it says here, one who is like this is "supreme." A guru who has these sorts of characteristics is of single form with all the Victorious Ones of the ten directions, a form that appears but has no true nature. Also, his body is not confusing. His speech is not blabber. His mind does not seem to be full of ideas. He does good works for the welfare of students who are so fortunate. The noble Nagarjuna proclaimed:

That which is the true nature of the Tathagata
Is the true nature of this living being.
The Tathagata has no true nature,
So this living being has no true nature.

In this manner, we will understand that we are essentially pure from the primordial, and are non-dual.
At all times, we must contemplate that they are before us, on the crowns of our heads, or are in the center of the lotus of our hearts. We present a

request to them that they pacify all the turmoil in the world and in its peace, so that we will acquire all the endowments of this world, and those that are beyond this world. Or we may meditate that they are non-dual with us. This is how we generate the conception that our guru is a Buddha, but the Sutra of the Invocations of Higher Consideration[31] proclaims:

> Maitreya, you must understand that the ones who teach what the Buddha proclaims are brave for four reasons. You may ask what these four are. Maitreya, they are brave because they have the meaning. They do not have what is meaningless. They have the Dharma. They do not have what is not the Dharma. They make our emotional problems diminish. They do not make them grow. They are teachers of the virtues and benefits of nirvana. They are not teachers of the virtues and benefits of samsara. These are the four.
>
> Maitreya, a son of heritage or daughter of heritage who is brave for these four reasons, or who becomes brave, will use their desires to generate a conception about the Buddha, and use it for a conception about their teacher. Then they must listen to the holy Dharma. You may ask why this is so. Maitreya, all those things that are somewhat well-spoken were spoken by the Buddhas.

In the above, it teaches that after we meditate on the Victorious Ones and their children we make offerings, but it does not speak about presenting our solicitations. Here, it proclaims that after we meditate on our gurus we present solicitations, but it does not speak about offerings. We must look back and forth among the scriptures, and understand that they exemplify each other.

This is the explanation of meditating with visualizations.

The noble Nagarjuna proclaimed:

> A summary of the embodiment of the Dharma
> Is that it is born from the king of wisdoms.

I then proclaim that we must meditate without visualizations in our efforts to attain an embodiment of the Dharma.

The root of all the dharmas:
Virtue, evil, happiness, sorrow,

---

[31] Lhag pa'i bsam pas bskul ba'i mdo

Likewise, samsara and nirvana,
Is our minds.

Virtue is from the word *kusala*. *Ku* means bad. *Sala* means to give up or throw off. In this case it is to give up. We give up things like taking lives and taking what is not given. Non-virtues are things like taking lives. Samsara is an idea. Nirvana is to be free from these. On this topic, master Dignaga proclaimed:

> Except for our ideas,
> There is nothing whatever that is called: "Samsara."
> When you are free from these ideas,
> You will be forever in nirvana.

The root of all these things is the mind. When our minds give up problematic activities, that is virtue. Not to give them up is evil. The mind that understands these things is in nirvana. If we do not understand, we are in samsara. On this topic, the Sutra that Removes All Obstructions Due to Karma[32] proclaims:

> Monks, what is this mind that when it is totally emotional, all sentient beings become totally emotional, and when this mind is pure, the sentient beings also become pure?

The Tantra on the True Enlightenment of Vairocana proclaims:

> Enlightenment is a comprehensive understanding
> Of the purity of our own minds,
> Just as they are.

The noble Nagarjuna also proclaimed:

> All things are just the mind.
> They occur to us properly,
> In the form of illusions.
> These are the karmas of virtue and non-virtue.
> Through them we are born in happy lives or horrible lives.

So you may ask: "If all the dharmas of samsara and nirvana are just the mind, won't that make it into a true entity?

---

[32] Las kyi sgrib pa thams cad rnam par dag pa'i mdo

When we make a thorough investigation of our mind,
In every way,
We see that it is not a color.
It is also not a shape.
It is not one.
It is not many.
For these reasons it is not an essence,
And therefore is not born.
It does not stay.
It does not stop.
It has no borders or center.
Its way of being is the uncomplicated sky.

The Tantra on the Condensation of Reality[33] proclaims:

Child of Heritage,
To individually understand our own minds,
We place ourselves into equanimity.

Now when we use study and contemplation to thoroughly investigate our minds, and comprehensively investigate them in meditation, we will find that they are not complicated, in the manner of the sky. For this reason, if they had been formed from some essence, if they were shaped into a form, they would need to have been formed by a color or a shape, but they are not formed by a color or a shape. The Words that Teach All the Tantras[34] proclaims:

What the mind is
Is essentially without roots,
Without basis,
Without a shape or color.
It transcends the senses.
It is not in the domain of our ideas.

You may ask: "Is it made of some essence other than form?"

It is not. If it were formed as an essence, it would indubitably require that it be formed as either one or many, but the mind is free from unity and plurality. This topic is discussed extensively later on, so I will not elaborate on it here.

[33] De nyid bsdus pa'i rgyud
[34] rGyud thams cad bstan pa'i tshig

Due to the fact that it is not formed as singular or plural, it has no essence, and because it has no essence, it is not born. If it were to be born, it would be born from a cause or would be born without a cause.

It is not reasonable that it was born from a cause. A cause and a result do not happen at the same time, so they do not meet. If they met, it would be absolutely certain that causes and results happen at the same time. If they happen at the same time, which is the cause of which? Which is the result of which?

It is also not reasonable that it be born from no cause. Things that have no cause are not to be observed coming from anything else, so the conclusion would be that they are permanently existent or that they are non-existent. Reason damages this idea.

Furthermore, it is not reasonable that something that exists be born, for it has already been formed. It is also not reasonable that a non-existent thing be born, for when there is no entity there can be no creation of a cause for it. On this topic, the noble Nagarjuna has also spoken:

> Things that exist exist,
> So they are not born.
> Things that do not exist do not exist,
> So they are not born.

Because things are not born, they do not remain, and because they do not remain, they do not end. They are free from birth at the beginning, staying in the present, and ceasing in the end. The Blessed One has also proclaimed in the Sutras:

> All dharmas lack defining characteristics.
> They are not born and they do not end.

You may ask: "What is this mind that does not exist as a truth, but is luminous and aware.

> *While this is so,*
> *Our awareness does not stop.*
> *This is the identity of awareness and emptiness.*

The mind is not made of any true essence, but is aware and has experiences. The awareness itself is essentially empty of any true nature. Emptiness is aware and luminous. Its identity is the interactivity of awareness and emptiness. The Victorious One's Sutras proclaim:

Consciousness is empty.
Emptiness is also conscious.
There is no consciousness other than emptiness.
There is also no emptiness other than consciousness.

So I show that our own minds are an interaction of awareness and emptiness, and then use this to show its exemplification in other beings:

The way it is with my mind
Is likewise the nature of the mind
For every sentient being,
And all the dharmas are also
An interaction of appearance and emptiness.
We ascertain this comprehensively,
And use a way in which we do not grasp
To settle ourselves into intense equanimity.

Just as my mind is an interaction of awareness and emptiness, the minds of every sentient being are also an interaction of awareness and emptiness. There is no difference in their true natures.

This is not only about the mind. All dharmas that appear as external objects, such as our bodies, are made of an interaction between appearance and emptiness. The Victorious One's Mother proclaims:

When we understand the way things are with consciousness,
We will understand all dharmas
In both their brevity and their vastness.

The Compiled Verses proclaims:

We understand that all sentient beings are just like ourselves.
We understand that all the dharmas are just like sentient beings.

Furthermore, the Heart of Wisdom proclaims:

Form is emptiness.
Emptiness is form.
Emptiness is not other than form.
Form is also not other than emptiness.

I this way, we become totally sure through our studies and contemplations that all dharmas are a non-dual interaction between appearance and emptiness, and when we meditate, we use the method of not holding onto any definitions about things, that they exist or do not exist, to place ourselves into deepest equanimity.

Once I have taught the method for placing ourselves into equanimity extensively, I follow up with a summary to teach the contemplation of placing ourselves into equanimity:

So we place ourselves into equanimity
In two ways that use visualizations,
Without visualizations,
And in a state of interaction,
So that without being pushed around by our ideas,
We come to attain the holy samadhi
Of peaceful abiding.

In the method described above, it is by cause of the two kinds of visualization, of a god or of a guru, and through placing ourselves in a non-conceptual samadhi that has no visualizations, that we get the result, a taking of the holy samadhi of peaceful abiding into our spirits.

You may ask what this samadhi is like. It is a samadhi that is not troubled by all our thoughts. The King of Samadhi proclaims:

Through the power of peaceful abiding
We will be unshakable.
Through higher vision we will be like mountains.
No sentient being will be able to bother us.
These have been described to be
The two kinds of patience.

Non-conceptual samadhi contradicts our ideas, so it is appropriate that we give them up. The two that employ visualizations are just ideas. So you may say: "If we are meditating on ideas, it is not appropriate that we reject ideas."

This is certainly true, but the use of visualizations and ideas is not truly contradictory. I myself do not want to truly give them up, and there will be no contradiction in transmitting them. Non-visualization itself is born out of the cause that we have had visualizations. On this topic, the Jewel Construction also proclaims:

In the same way that two pieces of wood,
When rubbed by the wind,
Produce fire,
And this fire burns them up,
We develop our knowledge and sensations,

But through this development they are burned up.

Lord Maitreya has also proclaimed:

One who relies on visualizations
Will develop non-visualization.
One who depends on non-visualization
Will brilliantly develop what is not to be visualized.

The Dharma Lord has also spoken on this:

We direct our minds toward the visualization itself,
And our thoughts achieve peace.
When we direct ourselves to the visualization itself,
We brilliantly avoid clinging to the visualization.

This is a good presentation on the way we place ourselves into equanimity.

Concerning the way we follow up, the Sutra on Inexhaustible Intellect proclaims:

We use our sense of memory
So that these Dharmas,
In which we practice a sense of diligence,
Will not be exhausted,
But will flourish.

This teaches that we must use our memory, so that our virtues are not exhausted but will grow.

We must repeatedly recollect the joy
That follows all our deeds,
Whether virtuous or evil,
And recall the virtuous,
So that we may augment its power
And make it increase.

This is to say: "We delight in virtue, so we must remember it."

You may ask: "What is the use of this requirement?"

Generally, when we delight in any virtue or evil that we do, and repeatedly call it to memory, the strength of what we have done is made to grow.

This should continue with:

We use our regrets about all the virtues and evils we have done,
Remembering them repeatedly.
The power of this makes things easy or obstructs things.
This is why we must regret our evils,
And eliminate them.

But this is the occasion to discuss the follow ups for virtues, so it is not actually included in the Root.
In general, we are advised to do a recollection after all virtues, but particularly, we must do a recollection after we place ourselves into equanimity.

After we have settled ourselves
Into a specific visualization,
We scrutinize the visualization,
The form,
And the meaning of our experience,
Individually,
And examine them thoroughly.
We examine their causes, conditions, other factors,
And the way they arise in dependencies,
In all their variety.
We scrutinize them until
We understand the meaning of what we see
Without visualizing anything
To practice a higher perception.

Generally speaking, we must remember every virtue. This is true, but the present occasion falls into a situation where we do this after placing ourselves into equanimity. This is why after we have placed ourselves into equanimity in a visualization on the body of the Buddha, or something similar, we particularly separate the object of our visualization, the form of our mind, this visualization's causes and conditions, as well as its form, and what the causes and conditions are for this experience, then we investigate them and make a detailed analysis.

When we do this, there are, relatively speaking, dependencies and connections to the causes and conditions of the visualization, in all their variety, so that we say: "This comes from that." We use the way of reversal of the way things occur in dependencies and connections, saying: "This was not made, so that was not made." We understand that the visualization and the form are Dharmas that, from the primordial, are not to be visualized at all, just as they are. We brilliantly achieve the wisdom of a higher perception.

Moreover, the Jewel Cloud of the Sutras proclaims:

Through peaceful abiding
We smash the heads of emotional problems.
Through higher perception
We bring emotional problems to an end.

Lord Maitreya has also proclaimed:

Through a stable peaceful abiding and higher perception
A yogin may go to every level.
He uses them for every practice.

You may ask: "Why is it that they are called peaceful abiding and higher perception?" Lord Maitreya has proclaimed:

Basing ourselves on a proper abiding,
We place our minds into our minds,
And brilliantly scrutinize the Dharmas.
For these reasons,
They are peaceful abiding and higher perception.

So after the instructions on what we must recollect so that our virtues will not be exhausted, but grow, there are the instructions on making a thorough dedication, so that they will not diminish.

We take them up as considerations, saying: "I must thoroughly dedicate them, and transform them." You may ask: "What is it that we are to dedicate?" The Buddha Avatamsaka proclaims:

The virtues of all living beings,
However many there may be,
And those we have done, will do, or are doing.

According to this method, we bind into one all the virtues of the three times, exemplifying them with the virtues that we are doing.

As for the time, we dedicate immediately after or upon doing the virtue. When we have done no virtue, there is nothing to dedicate. If we wait for a long time, there is the saying:

> All our good deeds,
> Such things as giving and making offerings to the Sugatas,
> Gathered through a thousand eons,
> Will be decimated by a single moment of anger.

There are a lot of conditions that cause the ruin of virtues that have not been dedicated, and they will be wasted during the interim.

Regarding who we do it for, the Victorious One's Mother proclaims:

> We do it in common with all sentient beings.

So we do it for ourselves and for all the abundant sentient beings.

Regarding the level of dedication, the Victorious One's Mother proclaims:

> We do not apply ourselves to make a dedication
> Toward the level of an Auditor,
> Or the level of a Private Buddha,
> But only toward omniscience itself.
> We make our dedication
> To the attainment of unsurpassed enlightenment.

You may ask: "What does it do when we make such dedications?"

In my concluding remarks you will see "inexhaustible" right at the end. This is because the virtue there is in a dedication toward magnificent enlightenment is made inexhaustible. The Sutra of Inexhaustible Intellect proclaims:

> A drop of water that falls in the great ocean
> Will not be exhausted
> For just so long as the ocean is not exhausted.
> In the same way,
> Virtues dedicated toward enlightenment
> Will not be exhausted
> For just so long as enlightenment is not exhausted,
> But also acts to guide us.

The possessions we get as a result of giving, the high status we get through the rule of the way, and such are real material things, so it is not necessary that we dedicate them. When we do evil, we may not dedicate it to hell, but we will be born there anyway. This is the same thing.

This being so, when we dedicate our generosity and other virtues towards causes for unsurpassed enlightenment, we get temporary results and ultimately, we achieve enlightenment. For this reason, our dedication guides us. When we are not sure where to go to get golden things, we are guided by the brilliant orations of others. This is the same thing. Master Singhabadra proclaimed:

> The act of dedication in our minds
> Is like an ornament made by a goldsmith.
> It acts as a facet toward
> Our complete and perfect enlightenment.

It also acts as a multiplier. The Great Perfection of Wisdom proclaims:

> Śāriputra,
> To continue,
> When a Bodhisattva,
> A Mahasattva,
> Gives even a small gift to any sentient being,
> He uses wisdom in methods,
> And dedicates it to omniscience itself.
> Those who wish to do
> Innumerable and incalculable virtues
> Must study the Perfection of Wisdom.

Now that I have explained that we dedicate so that our roots of virtue will not be exhausted, I will explain that before we have done a virtue we make a prayer so that the things we desire will come to pass. We have not, at that moment, gathered the virtue that we will transform. So we make a prayer in our thoughts: "Why shouldn't something happen that is both temporarily and ultimately of great purpose?" And with our voice we make a prayer: "May it be so." If we do this, the things we have prayed for will happen exactly as we have prayed for them.

You may ask why. It because of all the Dharmas of virtue and evil, of samsara and nirvana, the mind is primary. On this topic, the Removal of the Regrets of Ajātaśatru proclaims:

Through our prayers we will bring about a complete transformation.

The Jewel Construction also proclaims:

As everything there is is a condition,
It is consecrated in the roots of our yearnings.
One who makes a prayer
Will get a fruition of like kind.

If we are, at that moment, gathering the virtue that is to be transformed, and we say something while it is in vision, this is not a prayer that will work as a dedication. This being so, when the Prayer of Samantabhadra proclaims:

I will offer these to the Buddhas of the past,
And those who dwell in the ten directions of the world.

Such things are not prayers.

So you may think: "This must be because we have already gathered the virtues of the previous six branches [of the seven branches of worship] in the past." There is no problem here, for these are done while contemplating the transformation of virtues done previously, but it does not say this. The virtues that have come before are dedicated in the dedication that is the final branch. When we are not contemplating the transformation of virtues, whether or not they took place in the past, that is a prayer. So it is taught.

So after an extensive presentation on the way to do a follow up, there is a summary to show what is needed:

So it is that all our virtues,
Being ornamented by recollection.
Dedication, and holy prayers.
Are not exhausted,
But are augmented,
And become causes toward the magnificent objectives
Of everyone,
Ourselves and other beings.

In this way I advise you to augment every virtue, ornamenting it with a holy recollection, make every virtue inexhaustible, ornamenting it with a holy dedication, and make every virtue a great cause to benefit yourself and others, ornamenting it with a holy prayer. I advise you to use these three for your ornaments. These three are primary, but each of them also has the three aspects of inexhaustibility, augmentation, and the achievement of a great purpose, so if we describe them as being needed in common, there is no contradiction. Now all three of them are called holy. This is to avoid the recollection of regrets, the dedication toward perversity, and prayer for things that are wrong.

After showing the way to do a follow up, I present the way to stamp all things with a seal. To establish that relative reality is like an illusion, I say:

> *So these things that we take into our experience,*
> *As well as compounded dharmas in all their variety,*
> *All depend on causes and conditions,*
> *And are not made out of their own essences.*

Things that depend on causes and conditions are not made through their own essential nature, and even the twelve Dharmas for taking things into our experience, such as the moon in the water, depend on causes and conditions. Not only that, there are no compounded dharmas that are made from their own essential natures. On this topic, the Questions of the Naga King Avatapta proclaims:

> Things that are born through conditions
> Are not born.
> There is no true being whatsoever
> That would give birth to them.
> Things that depend on conditions
> Are described as empty.
> One who understands emptiness
> Is conscientious.

But even though they are not made from any true essence, I use an analogy to show how this does not interrupt the aspect of their appearance:

> *They appear in various ways*
> *To our polluted minds,*
> *Due to our habits.*
> *These experiences are not true.*
> *We contemplate that they are like illusions*
> *That have occurred through a variety of conditions,*
> *Or are like dreams that are mixed into our sleep.*

Although they are not made of a true essence, the mind that has been mixed up through beginningless time by a multitude of habitual patterns, including external objects, inner consciousness, the running of consciousness toward objects, and the craving for this, perceives external objects that are attractive or unattractive, and experiences a variety of things within, such as happiness and sorrow, but these are not true. Master Nagarjuna's Mind Commentary proclaims:

> Relative reality is born out of emotional problems and karma.
> Karma comes from the mind.
> Habitual patterns are amassed from out of the mind.
> The exhaustion of habitual patterns is the finest happiness.

They come from a variety of conditions, and appear as a variety of things. An analogy is that it is like an illusion in which mud, gravel, a monkey's tail and other ingredients, through the use of specific mantras, appear to be a multitude of horses, oxen, and other animals. We must understand this. The Lord of the Logicians has proclaimed:

> As an analogy,
> To those whose senses are confused by things like mantras,
> Things like mud and plates
> Are obviously something else,
> Even though there is no connection to their form.

The King of Samadhi proclaims:

> The illusionists project their illusions
> And make assortments of horses, oxen, and chariots.
> There is nothing whatever that is true about them.
> You must understand that all dharmas are just the same.

A mind that is mixed up by habitual patterns will experience a variety of things. An analogy is that this is like a person whose dreams are mixed up with sleep. They will experience a variety of things, but they are not true. The King of Samadhi proclaims:

> This is like the arrival of boyfriend
> In the dreams of a young woman,
> Who then sees him die.
> When he arrives she is delighted.
> When he dies she is unhappy.
> You must understand that all dharmas are like that.

You may be thinking: "We may conclude that there is no truth to compounded dharmas, but uncompounded dharmas, such as the sky and cessation, are true. So I say:

Uncompounded dharmas are nothing but attributions.
The sounds of meaningless words
Are compounded by our conceptualizations.
Those who believe they are meaningful
Are mad.

Entities that are not compounded from causes and conditions, such as the sky, are nothing but ideas. They are not truly real. If they were truly real, how would we understand them? If they are to be understood by the direct perception of the senses or the mind, then the uncompounded would turn out to be an object of our five senses, such as a form. If they were made from our experience, they would turn out to be our minds. It is also impossible to prove their existence by inference. This is because there is no connection whatever between being uncompounded and being a dharma. Therefore, the sound when we say "uncompounded" is nothing but a dharma compounded to be an object for our minds. This being so, anything that we wish would signify the uncompounded is nothing but an insane attribution for the way things are.

So you may be thinking: "Well, as dharmas that are compounded and uncompounded are not true, it will follow that there is no happiness or sorrow that results from virtue and evil, and this being so, it will follow that there is no need to work on taking things up or relinquishing them. To prevent these reverted ideas, I say:

The dependent origin of relative causes and conditions
Is not a deception.
We will experience the full fruition
Of the things that we do.
We must, therefore, not ignore
The way of causes and conditions.

Ultimately, karma and the fruits of karma are not real, and there is nothing to apprehend for acquisition or relinquishment, but in relative reality there is no deception in the dependent and connected occurrence by which preceding causes bring forth subsequent results. Through the full maturation of the virtuous and non-virtuous karmas that we do, we will experience happiness and sorrows, just as you see. For this reason, we must not ignore the causes and results of karma.

The Sutras also proclaim:

Our karmas will not decompose,
Even in a hundred eons.
When they find their associations and their time,
They will ripen into results for those who have bodies.

The noble Nagarjuna has also proclaimed:

Our blessed gurus have spoken on
The abode of karma,
The identity of karma,
The fruition of karma,
The personal karmas of sentient beings,
And on karma's not decomposing.

Now the belief that because the doer of the karma experiences its maturation, there must be something called an inconceivable self that is eternal, that is a single thing that is a doer of karma and an experiencer of its maturation, is a reverted idea. This is what is taught. I say:

To want it to be true that things exist
Is a way of seeing things as permanent.

This sort of eternal self would not be changed by conditions.

Through virtuous karma we will experience happiness,
And through non-virtuous karma
We will generate a result of sorrow.

The glorious Dharmakirti has proclaimed:

This is a cause that gives birth to sorrow.
It is a fetter.
If it is permanent,
What will be the cause so that sorrow is not born?
It will be freedom.
Investigate it, and where it comes from.

This being so, those who hold to these sort of views may have vowed that the Buddha is their teacher, but they are going in the opposite direction of the teachings of the Buddha. They are no different than the heterodox.

So once I have explained stamping relative reality with the seal that it is like an illusion, I describe stamping ultimate reality with the seal that it has no true nature. I say:

> *There are no dharmas that do not have a time and place.*
> *When we separate them according to their time and place,*
> *It will be impossible for there to be a solitary entity.*
> *There is no one,*
> *So where will the many come from?*
> *There is also nothing that is other than these.*
> *So saying: "They exist"*
> *Is a miserable idea.*

There are a lot of established conclusions that profess on entities, this is true, but once we advocate an entity that is true, we resolve that objects and understandings are a duality. It is not possible that there be objects that have no position, or understandings that have no time. If we subdivide positions and times, believing that minute atoms which have no parts are the ultimate reality, our view is that subtle atoms coalesce.

But when they are assembled into a rough form, where one partless minute atom in the middle is suddenly joined with six atoms in the six directions, there will be a place where each of the atoms join. The central minute atom will have six parts, and in the place where it joins with the atom to the east, it will also be joined to the other five. So a dense atom will become the same size as a minute atom. If this were so, there would be no conglomeration into gross form. This was discussed by Master Vasubhandu:

> If the six were suddenly joined,
> The most minute atoms would have six parts.
> But if these six were in one place,
> Even a lump would turn out to be a minute atom.

So it is that when we divide them by place it is impossible that there be one atom, and so there will be no multitude of them to be assembled. Therefore, external objects are not formed.

Further, if our view is to believe that knowledge that is instantaneous and has no parts is the ultimate truth, then this knowledge which is instantaneous and has no parts will not have the parts of birth, destruction, and continuation, and it will turn out that it is not compounded.

If it does have them, every instant will turn out to have three parts, and there will be no one thing. It will also turn out that pluralities do not come about, for there will be nothing to hold them together. This is what the noble Nagarjuna discussed in his Rosary of Jewels:

> As instants have ends,
> We must determine that they have beginnings and middles.
> So an instant will have three identities.
> Therefore,
> The world does not remain even for an instant.

Further, when an instant that has no parts moves from the former into the latter, it will turn out that unless it touches on these two instants it has no cause. If they touch, it will turn into both the part that is connected to the former and the part that is connected to the latter, and so the part that is connected to the former is also connected to the latter. If they are connected at the same time, the previous instant will remain throughout the three times. If they are connected at different times, the middle instant will turn out to exist in two times. This is because the instant of time that is connected to the former will not discontinue in the time that is connected to the latter.

For these reasons, it is impossible that there be an entity that is a single instant, and if there is not one, how could there be many? Through using time to divide things in this way, we will also prove that even the mind has no true nature.

Something else, that is neither an object nor a knowledge, does not exist any more than the one-hundredth part of the tip of a hair. Objects and knowledge are disproven by reason. Therefore, ideas that say: "It exists" are simply a lack of scrutiny and are nothing but the miserable attitudes that are popular.

After I describe the refutation of the extreme position that things exist, I demonstrate a refutation of the extreme position that they do not exist.

> *If nothing were long,*
> *How could anything be short?*
> *Existence is not made up out of any essence.*
> *So how could there be a view*
> *In which non-existence is natural?*

You may ask: "You have refuted existence, so are things non-existent?"

They are not. The thing called "non-existence" requires that we refer to an existence. Existence is not made through any real essence, so while we may look for a nature or true essence for non-existence, where would it be? An analogy is that if there is no distance in our vision, there would not be a nearness in reference to it. Furthermore, when we do a bit of investigation of what it is that is non-existent when we say: "It does not exist." We will not find anything. So where would this non-existence be? On this topic, master Jñānagarbha has proclaimed:

> The thing we would negate
> Does not exist.
> It is obviously not to be negated,
> When we are correct.

The noble Nagarjuna also proclaimed:

> For this reason,
> The Buddhas have described this undying teaching
> That is beyond existence and non-existence
> As "profound."
> You must know it to be the purse of the Dharma.

The third heap is the refutation:

> *We make things clear*
> *With these two disparaging observations:*
> *That neither a thing to prove nor a referent exists.*
> *There are no dharmas that both exist and do not exist,*
> *And there are none that are neither.*
> *You must use a clear wisdom to understand this.*

You may ask: "Is a heap that is both of them the third?

It is not. Both existence and non-existence have already been elucidated through spoken logic. It is also not the non-existence of something that is both existent and non-existent, for there is no logic to prove this. If it were not either of them it would be necessary that they refer to something that is both of them, and neither of their referents exist, so how would there be a reality that is neither of them?

In this way, you, O King of shining wisdom, must understand that we reject these four extreme positions and are free from their complications.

Now it is certainly true that we refute all the established conclusions that profess entities, but we especially refute even the greatest of the great views of the Nyāya, for they are actually just obsessions.

If our idea is that
Because the mind has no form,
It has no place,
And therefore it is true that it is solitary,

The Nyāya says that because the mind has no form, the logic by which we attribute six sides to something does no damage, and because the past and the future are not made of entities, the reason by which we scrutinize three times does no damage. They have the idea that only the mind in the present, without instants or parts, is true. I present a refutation of this:

Then there will be
Both taking in and holding onto a multiplicity of appearances
And oneness,
So our minds will also be multiple.
We will turn out to be liars.

Here I am showing the refutation to be primary. Is the appearance of subjects and objects in a multitude of forms a single partless knowledge, or is it diverse? If it is single, in the way of the Satyākārins, this knowledge will turn out to be multiple. This is because the plurality and the self would be the same. For those who profess a Dharma that has this position, that which encompasses is multiple, while it is the self alone, but this is a plurality. An analogy is that the impermanences of a pillar and of a pot are different. On this topic, The Treasure of Logical Reason proclaims:

When we look outside,
The objects of our awareness are multiple.
When we look inward,
They are one in self-awareness.

This states that even though things appear to be multiple when we look outwards, they are one in self-awareness when we look inward. This statement is based on the Nyāya tradition. If this were not so, it would be disproven by the logic that negates the possession of branches.

When we envision a shifting appearance of white and a stable appearance of yellow at the same time, and when we look outward there is the shifting appearance of white, then when we look inward, even our self-awareness will shift. This is because the shifting and the self would be the same. This being so, even the yellow that appears to be stable when we look outward will be shifting. This is because the shifting self-awareness and the self would be the same. If you accept this, what will prevent the eventuality that just because the stable appearance of yellow and the self are the same, even the shifting appearance of white will be stable?

You may say: "Both the appearance of stability and of shifting are delusions, for in truth they are the mind."

This requires that we determine that the mind is made from a foundational entity that is neither stable nor instable. No matter how we advocate this understanding, we will be accepting something that is unacceptable, so what is there to refute?

Now according to the way of liars, consciousness is a lie. This is because lies appearing in a variety of forms and the self are one.

Now I present my final refutation:

Where does the appearance of duality come from?
What about nirvana being the exhaustion of delusion?

According to the Satyākārins, a variety of things appears, but in reality they are self-awareness's external control. This is the rationale by which they appear as a variety of things, but it will not be acceptable that they are a fully established reality that has not been composed of subjects and objects from the primordial. Our consciousness of the appearance of a variety of things is on account of our accepting that the subject that has external control is different than self-awareness.

If the appearance of a variety of things and our consciousness are different, it will not turn out to be possible that they appear as dual. This is because different things are not connected at the same time.
You may be thinking: "The appearance of duality is a delusion, and so is not real, but it appears by force of our habitual tendencies."

You are only thinking of the differences. The appearances are not real. This non-reality is beyond the designations of single and multiple. Furthermore, a fully established reality negates an attributed reality that surmounts the subject's external control, which is to be refuted. But this is unacceptable, for we cannot refute the appearance of a variety of things.

If it is the case that at the time we attain nirvana our delusions will be exhausted and this will stop the appearance of a variety of things, then the wisdom that is knowledge of what must be known in all its variety will be non-existent.

In these ways I refute the positions of others in a detailed explanation, then I present a final summary of the refutations:

> *Our taking things in is not made from any essentiality.*
> *Our holding on also has no essentiality.*
> *Those who claim that there is a true luminous awareness*
> *That is other than these,*
> *That is different from these transformations,*
> *Are totally lying to both themselves and others.*

The investigation through reason in the above shows that there is no one who takes things in who is made of an essential reality, as so there is also essentially no one who holds onto things. This is because holding on is done in reference to taking in. This is like the way that a consciousness of holding on to something as being white does not occur if there is nothing that is white.

When we look at those who believe that even though there are no subjects or objects, there is truly a luminous awareness that is other than them, there is no validity to what they are trying to prove. These views are damaged by such insights as that there is no unity or plurality.

The Samkhyas say that there is a soul that is different from twenty-two transformations. It is permanent, so there are twenty-four. But they have nothing to establish their belief in an eater or one who enjoys. This view is damaged by the fact that something permanent must be either gradual or instant, and by emptiness.

People who advocate these kinds of things are the greatest liars.

So now that I have refuted the investigations made by others, I present the way things are in ultimate reality:

> *There is no essentiality that is unborn from the primordial.*
> *You must comprehensively understand all dharmas*
> *In their true nature,*
> *Which is entirely free from complications,*
> *Then let yourself be without visualizations,*
> *Like the sky.*

From the primordial, no dharmas, whether compounded or uncompounded, have been born, so they have no true nature. Once you understand that they are naturally free from all the indicators of complications, such as being existent or non-existent, you will stamp them with the seal of non-visualization, as if they were the sky. On this topic, the Compiled Verses proclaims:

> Once we have used wisdom to decimate dharmas,
> Be they compounded, uncompounded, white, or black,

We will not envision even an atom.
When the world is pure,
We will go to the city of the perfection of wisdom.

Lord Maitreya proclaimed:

There is nothing to clear away here.
There is not a single thing that we must put down.
We look purely at purity itself.
When we see the purity,
We are fully liberated.

Once I have explained that we stamp ultimate reality with the seal of its being without a true nature, I present a teaching on stamping them both with the seal of interactivity:

We also do not reject the way
Of the emptiness of all dharmas.
We do not cut off the flow
Of dependent and connected origination.
This is a miracle.
When we understand these things
It will be more than amazing.
It will be extremely amazing.

When we thoroughly understand the way in which all the dharmas of samsara and nirvana are empty of any essential truth, we will not reject them, for in relative reality there is an uncut current of the dependent and connected occurrence of causes and results, just as it appears. This is the miraculous Dharma of the interactivity of the two truths.

The knowledge that things are like this is the most amazing of all the things that are amazing. The noble Nagarjuna has proclaimed:

That which occurs through dependencies and connections
Is explained to be emptiness.

He also proclaimed:

For the reason that there are not any dharmas that exist
That are not originated in dependencies,
There are not any dharmas
That are not empty.

You may ask: "What is the way of interactivity like?"

You must understand
That all objects are an interactivity
Of appearance and emptiness,
That our minds are also an interactivity
Of awareness and emptiness,
That our path is an interactivity
Of methods and wisdom,
And you must totally immerse yourself in this
In all things.

You must understand that while all objects, such as forms, appear, they are empty of any true nature, like the moon in the water. The King of Samadhi proclaims:

When the moon rises up in a shimmering sky
And form appears on a shimmering lake,
The moon has not moved into the water.
You must understand that all dharmas are just so.

Everything in our minds, the consciousness in our eyes and all the rest, is evident and we are aware of it, but it is empty of any true nature. We must understand that this is like the consciousness we experience in our dreams. The Victorious One's Mother proclaims:

Consciousness is like a dream.
It is like an illusion.

We must understand that all the pathways of peaceful abiding, higher perception, and the rest, are an interactivity of methods and wisdom, like the wheels of a chariot. If we have no methods, we will fall into the extreme of nirvana. If we have no wisdom, we will fall into samsara. We will not be able to travel to the city of the nirvana that is not in stasis. This is like having a chariot that has no wheels. We will not move on. A Sutra proclaims:

Wisdom that has no method is a fetter.
Method that has no wisdom is also a fetter.

Another Oration by this magnificent personage proclaims:

Wisdom that has no methods
Is the enemy of all our virtues.
Methods that have no wisdom
Do not liberate us.

After a detailed presentation, I finish up with a final summary by offering advice:

Dependent origination is relative,
Totally obfuscated,
Like an illusion.
Its true nature is ultimate,
The holy intent,
Emptiness.
There is no separation between these two.
They are interactive.
You must understand all the Dharmas,
Of cause, path, and fruition.

In relative reality, the things that occur through dependencies and connections appear to us as illusions, while in ultimate reality they are empty of any true nature. These two are not separate. That which appears is empty of any truth. That which is empty appears without hindrance. They are interactive. All the Dharmas of samsara and nirvana, which are our cause, are stamped with this seal. This is a true certification that endures.

It is by this very cause that all paths, such as that of the six perfections, are stamped with this seal: We take meditation into our experience by not conceptualizing the three spheres: The giver, the gift, and the recipient.

All our results, such as our physical embodiment, are stamped with the seal of the natural embodiment of the Dharma. This is the certification of the result that we achieve.

I advise you, O Lord of the Earth, to understand that this is the way of all Dharmas, be they causes, paths, or fruitions.

Once I have made a detailed presentation on the way we take these things into our experience, I present a concluding summary to bring together the totality of the path of virtue:

So it is that these five:
The basis, preliminaries, placing ourselves in equanimity,
The follow-up tasks, and the stamping of all things with a seal,
Completely subsume all the Dharmas of virtue.

According to the way that is discussed above, there is the basis of the path: The pure rule of the way; the preparation for the path: A contemplation on our motivations; the actual practice of the path: The yoga of placing ourselves into equanimity; the methods for augmenting the virtues of the path: Recollection, and the stamping of the path and every Dharma with a seal.

Each has three parts,
When divided up,
There are fifteen.

They entirely subsume all the proclamations on the practice of the path of virtuous karma that are found in the Sugata's Orations, however many there may be. For this reason, I show that we must be complete in all the Dharmas of virtue:

One who perseveres at all these ways of the Dharma,
In each of these enumerations of the path of virtue,

The extra word "do" must be added on here.

Regarding an account of virtuous practices, an example would be the seven branches of Dharma practice, which begin with offerings.
At the beginning, our basis is a completely pure rule of the way, by which we do not practice evil and we do practice virtue. When we have understood the special qualities of our guru and the precious ones, we will have faith, and we will have an urgent desire to make offerings and all the rest. We will perceive that we ourselves and other beings who have not yet achieved the kind of virtues the precious ones have are miserable. We will be motivated by a compassion that is a desire to free them of this. We visualize a resemblance of the special qualities of our guru and the precious ones, then we do the seven branches systematically.

We scrutinize the nature of the act of offering, the things that we offer, and all the rest. We understand that they are not true. There is no object whatever that is real. We settle into an equanimity in which our minds are not thinking of anything. Then we follow up by carefully scrutinizing all our previous acts of virtue. We recollect them with delight. Then we dedicate them to unsurpassed enlightenment. We say a prayer for our temporary and ultimate objectives.

Then I say: "You must stamp all of the Dharmas that you have already taken into your experience with the seal by which their appearance has no true nature."

Advice to Kublai Khan

Once I have presented the way that we must practice, I discuss the results of this practice:

We will enjoy all the happiness of high status,

A person who takes things into their experience in this way will maintain the rule of the way very purely, and will use holy prayers to properly adorn it. By doing this alone, we will attain the holy status of being a god or a human, so there is no need to mention our pleasure when everything is complete. Not only do we achieve true highness, we also achieve the holy status of true goodness. I say:

He will brilliantly gather up an oceanic collection
Of the two accumulations of merit and wisdom.
He will join himself to the path of nobles
With a clear samadhi.
He will make his wisdom grow
With meditation and practice.
He will use the ends of the path
To reach the end.

This verse presents our temporary fruitions. For one incalculable eon we accumulate a very vast store of merit and wisdom, so that our spirit is well filled with virtuous Dharmas. We maintain the samadhi of the four proximate recollections. We use the four correct relinquishments to build on our diligence. We use the four magical feet to make all this manifest, and we maintain the samadhi of the river of the Dharma. We make offerings to innumerable Buddhas, and listen to their Dharmas. We make our minds fit for work. This is the path of accumulation. The Ornament of the Sutras proclaims:

They will surely come to us for innumerable eons,
And make our wishes prosper everywhere.
Just as the water makes up the ocean,
We are fully perfected in the Dharmas of virtue.

After that, we immerse ourselves in the wisdom that the worldly get through meditation on the magnitude of what they have understood through study and contemplation. Then we develop clear vision through the samadhi in which the person that has a material form, the person who has a character, and every subject and object are all without any true nature.

We relinquish the thirty-seven kinds of conceptualizations. We are empowered into faith, perseverance, recollection, samadhi, and wisdom. We will have the power to overcome lack of faith, laziness, forgetfulness, mental disturbances, and distorted thinking. Our premonitions about the fire of non-conceptual wisdom will be warm. We will have patience for profound Dharmas, for they are the summit of the things that destabilize our roots of virtue, while they do not lead to evil rebirths.

This is the most excellent Dharma for the world. We apply ourselves to this noble path, in keeping with the parts of it that have been definitively discriminated, so it is the path of application. Maitreya's Ornament of the Sutras proclaims:

> So it is that after we have stopped our engagement in them,
> We relinquish all the disturbances that come from holding on,
> And as we gradually understand these things,
> We become warm, and all the rest.
> This is said to be so.

Right at the moment that follows, we give birth to a wisdom that conceptualizes sixteen aspects to the four truths, and by the power of seeing a reality that we had not seen before, we cut off our emotional and intellectual obstructions, our attributions and dormant tendencies, at the roots. We become more noble than ordinary individuals, and are ornamented with the seven branches of enlightenment, the wonders of a pathway that goes beyond the world. This is the path of seeing. It was discussed by Maitreya in his Ornament of the Sutras:

> Then by this,
> There is an unsurpassed wisdom
> That transcends the world.
> It is not an idea.
> It is stainless.
> We achieve freedom from the two kinds of holding on.

Through seeing this we get a wisdom that gives rise to a meditation that is beyond this world. We use it to settle into equanimity for two incalculable eons. We practice having no outflows, and we immerse ourselves in purity. We have reverence for follow-up practices. We dedicate and rejoice. We immerse ourselves in things that do not have outflows, and in nine progressive states, beginning with the smallest of the small, we develop our path of meditation. This vision progressively clears away the nine darknesses, beginning with the greatest of the great, which are synchronously created emotional and intellectual problems. Then we actually proclaim the multitude of virtues there are in the eightfold noble path. Our wisdom on the path of meditation grows higher and higher.

At the end of this we use the vajra-like samadhi to reach the end. We achieve the level of Buddhahood.

On this topic, the Ornament of True Understanding[35] proclaims:

On the ninth level,
The path is one in which
The smallest of the small,
And all the rest,
Are remedies for the pollution
Of the greatest of the great,
And all the rest.
It is pure.

Now the four that I have been discussing make us go higher and higher, so they fit the definition of a path. The path that reaches the end is a fruition, so it is only attributed to be a path. It is a level because it is a basis for Dharmas of virtue. I have spoken on this in detail in my letter called A Rosary of Gemstones,[36] so I will not talk about it here.

After my discussion of temporary results, I teach on ultimate results:

The true nature of the mind
Is to be primordially pure.
Its taste is one with its dominion,
In the pacification of our ideas.
When we understand its natural embodiment:
The wisdom of the dominion of the Dharma,
And a perfect store of renunciation,
As they are,

Here, the embodiment is the first thing presented. It is a natural embodiment, so we do not abide in it. The true nature of our minds has been pure from the primordial. When we fully pacify the façade of ideas, we will see our own wisdom very well by ourselves, like pouring water into water, or pouring oil into oil. The unity of our dominion and our wisdom is the embodiment of our true nature. This is also the wisdom of the dominion of the Dharma.

---
[35] mNgon par rtogs pa'i rgyan
[36] sPring yig nor bu phreng ba

From the word *Buddha* we get *Buddha puruṣa nidra prabuddha*, which is translated as: "The Buddha has awakened from the sleep of non-awareness, and so he is like a person who has woken from sleep." This is the perfect store of renunciation. This is also the knowledge of what is to be understood, just as it is. On this topic, the Ornament of True Understanding proclaims:

> The embodiment of the Sage's true essence
> Is the attainment of an inexhaustible Dharma
> That is perfect in every way,
> And fits the definition of a true nature.

The second Dharma is that our teacher uses the path to transform the Dharmas of samsara:

> *The Dharmas of samsara*
> *Are brilliantly transformed by the path.*
> *Our bodies transform in station,*
> *Into bodies arrayed with markings and exemplary features.*
> *Our speech transforms in station,*
> *Into a speech that has sixty cadences.*
> *Our minds transform in station,*
> *Into three wisdoms that hold knowledge*
> *Of how things are accounted for.*
> *Our problems are transformed in station,*
> *Into opportunities for the Victorious One,*
> *Our bountiful father.*
> *This is our embodiment in perfect pleasure.*

White cotton is transformed by dyes, to display a variety of colors. Just so, the Dharmas of samsara are transformed by the dye of the path. On the level of the Buddha, the wisdom of total liberation is displayed in everything we may know. The Ornament of the Sutras proclaims:

> Just as a cloth will display or not display the dye color
> Due to the particularities of the knot,
> The wisdom of liberation will be displayed or not displayed
> Due to the power of our projections.

As it says, our bodies transform in station into bodies that are embellished by the thirty-two good signs and eighty exemplary features. Our speech is transformed in station, to arise as a melodious voice that has sixty cadences. Our minds transform in station, and all these inexhaustible dharmas appear as if they were images in a mirror. This is the mirror-like wisdom. When our hearts are calm about samsara and nirvana, that is the wisdom of equanimity. The knowledge that comprehensively perfects all the Dharmas, without mixing them up, is the wisdom of discrete ideas. The problems there are in bad times for ordinary people are transformed, and arise as opportunities for the Victorious One, our bountiful father.[37]

So it is that through eternal time he teaches the Mahayana Dharma to his entourage of Bodhisattvas who abide on the levels, and with his children he has the perfect pleasure of inexhaustible bliss. For this reason he is an embodiment of perfect pleasure. On this topic, the ornament of True Understanding proclaims:

> He is a being with thirty-two marks.
> His exemplary features are eighty.
> He takes true pleasure in the Mahayana.
> This is why we believe him to be
> The embodiment of the Sage's perfect pleasure.

To teach the third body:

> *Our karma transforms in station,*
> *Into the wisdom that gets things done,*
> *And a vast account of good works.*
> *This is our manifest embodiment.*

Our karma transforms in station, and without our thinking about it, we work for the welfare of sentient beings. This is the wisdom that gets things done. Just as it is said:

> He forever teaches the craftsmen and the people
> About great enlightenment and nirvana.
> This is the Buddha's manifest embodiment.
> It is a magnificent means for total liberation.

A teacher who trains anyone, whoever they may be, among the three groups of impure disciples is a manifest embodiment of the Buddha.

Regarding the two kinds of physical embodiment, the word *Budha* is explained as: *Budha prabuddhata padma buddhavat*, which may be translated as: "A Buddha has an open mind regarding what may be known, like a lotus in bloom." It is also a full store of understanding.

---

[37] Pha mtha' yas

You may ask: "Just how long does this perfect store of fruitions last?" So I say:

He is endowed with empowerment,
So is eternal.
His river is not dammed.

It is because the Buddha is endowed with empowerments into the ten powers, which begin with life and karma, that he is eternal and his river is not dammed. On this topic, the Holy Golden Light proclaims:

The Buddha does not pass into nirvana.
The Dharma will not fail.
It is in order to assist the lazy
That his manifestations show the way to pass on.

Another source says:

Some pass into nirvana, like fire.
Some become enlightened Buddhas.
It is not the case
That the eternal embodiment of the Tathagata
Never existed.

The Ocean of Melodious Praise, which is an oration by this same great personage, proclaims:

The aspect of the virtues there are
To this ocean of wonders
Does not decline.
In view of death and passing on,
Where would it go?
This is certainly true,
But it appears to rise and set
On the mountain of those who are to be trained.

After I have presented the full store of virtues there are in our fruition, I give advice for practice:

I beg you, Lord of the People,
To forever and with no disruption
Employ yourself like this.

This is to say: "You, O Lord of the People, must persevere at these fifteen Dharmas, by way of taking them into your experience, and you will attain a fruition of the three embodiments along with their good works."

I am actually advising the King, but I am also advising others who are to be trained through its transmission. This is the same as the Buddha's Advice to King Bimbisara and Master Nagarjuna's Advice to King Gautamiputra. The Rosary of Precious Jewels proclaims:

> It is not certain that this teaching
> Is exclusively for the Dharma King.
> I have taught it with a wish that it be of benefit
> To other beings, as is reasonable.

After I have presented the actual content, I conclude by presenting a dedication:

> *Through the virtue there is*
> *In summarizing the profound intent*
> *Of the highest vehicle,*
> *And offering it to the people of the Dharma,*
> *May all living beings,*
> *With you being foremost, O King,*
> *Attain the holy status of Buddhahood.*

What is it they are to attain? The holy status of Buddhahood. Who will attain it? Sentient beings, among whom you, O King, are foremost. You may ask: "What will we depend on?" We will bring the meanings of this supreme vehicle's profundities together, and we will use the virtues there are in offering this to the people of the Dharma

When we use this vehicle to move forward, it is a causal vehicle. Here, we are moving forward with the vehicle of our fruition. Both of them are here.

Supreme means that this is specifically superior to the vehicles of the Auditors and the Private Buddhas.

So does this book bring together the orations of all the Sugatas, or does it bring together only the Mahayana? "Which is it," you may ask.

It brings together all of the Sugata's orations, but it brings them together into the Mahayana. This is so stated, and there are no contradictions. The Tantra on the Net of Magical Illusion proclaims:

> The appearance of the three vehicles is sure,
> But there is only one vehicle

In which we abide in our result.

In another book by this same great personage,[38] the Letter to Prince Mono Khan, this is proclaimed:

We do not attain great liberation
Elsewhere than the Mahayana.
So let your heart flow in the Mahayana,
And let it be a comfort to you.

It says "profound" because this is difficult for the childish, the Auditors, and the Private Buddhas to understand.

I teach this in summary form, so that the king will comprehend it with his sharp senses. It is proper that I offer a life of Dharma to the king.

As for pleasures, the king can, himself, vie with Vaiśāvaṇa in them, and even an animal can offer you a life of extravagance.

After I have presented my advice on the Dharma, I have an occasion to address casual concerns:

By offering this Excellent Work,
On the life of the Dharma,
The bravery in my mind grows,
O Lord of the People.
So I beg you to contemplate these few solicitations
Right from the start and without delay.

I present this as in invitation for you to listen to this, so I have contemplated in my thoughts that it is improper to say things that upset the hearts of the greatest of the great. You may ask where my bravery to do this comes from.

Through offering you this brilliant exposition on living the life of the Dharma my mind grows even more brave, and I beg you to listen to it a little, for your own sake as well as for others, and to contemplate it without being distracted when you have a little time.

After the invitation to listen to this, I make a recommendation for the welfare of the king himself:

Now is the time for you
To lengthen the lifespan of your body,
To support the glory of your lineage and your descendants,
And to persevere at these methods for finding total freedom.

---

[38] This refers to Chogyal Phagpa. The text here uses the voice of the editor.

Advice to Kublai Khan

It is fitting that you persevere at them without delay.

The time for you to persevere at methods that will lengthen your own life, stabilize the glory of your lineage and your descendants, and let you find total liberation, is now. It is appropriate that you persevere, without being distracted. This is what I said. I would add: "You yourself, O King, must begin right now to persevere at methods for lengthening your own life."

You may ask what these methods are.

My Letter to Prince Mono Khan proclaims:

To slaughter sentient beings who do no harm,
To scorn non-human beings,
And to discontinue holiday ceremonies:
These are the three causes
For the exhaustion of our lives.

So you must persevere at rejecting these things, at setting free those who are to be killed, and at maintaining holiday proceedings, among other things.

In this same way, there are methods to make the glory of your lineage and your descendants stable:

Through persevering for others we achieve our own desires.
Through protecting others we make offerings to ourselves.
Through speaking pleasantly we praise ourselves.
This is the technique for Dharmas that are real.

You must persevere at such methods as they are found in the commentaries:

By relying on the boat of humanity
We cross over the great river of sorrow.
It will be difficult to find this boat in the future.
When you are confused,
Do not go back to sleep.

We use such techniques as methods for reaching total liberation, so the time to persevere is right now.

You have acquired a faultless body that has both leisure and endowments. This is because you have met up with the teachings of the Buddha, and you have been taken in by very pure companions in virtue. The King of Samadhi proclaims:

> Two young men who were monks endowed with miraculous powers and supernatural cognition gave advice to the great king over Jambu Island. This is their advice to the king:

Listen, O Descendant of Kings!
It is very difficult to find the excellence
In the appearance of a Buddha.
The lords of the earth must always be conscientious.
Life is always moving and is not static.
It goes quickly,
Like a river on a mountain.
There is disease, sorrow, and the torture of old age.
You will get no other chance like this
To do virtuous karma.

I encourage you toward the grand objectives of the Dharma:

The glory of the Dharma that we teach has not failed,
And we have a Dharma King such as yourself.
This is an opportune time for those who wear saffron.
What do you feel about them in your heart?

The glory of the holy Dharma, the teachings of our teacher, the Buddha, has not failed, and there is a Dharma King such as yourself that is still alive, protecting the kingdom in keeping with the Dharma, someone who studies the teachings of our teacher. Yet those who hold the royal banner of saffron are being harmed by the commoners, and this is a situation where emotional problems prevail. How could your heart be equanimous about this? The Root Tantra of Mañjuśrī proclaims:

The aforementioned two monks gave advice to the king:

The king's elephants fulfill the Dharma.
They guard the teachings that hold ten powers.
When we are most afraid
That the time of our extinction is on us,
The king takes the side of the elephants of the Dharma.

The ordained are the roots of the Dharma, so it is appropriate that you consider them. This is what I ask you to do.

In particular, I exhort you on my own behalf:

I am not old in my age,
But my body's strength has diminished,
And my mind is slack with a casual attitude.
For these reasons,
I am seeking out a secluded place
To pursue the intent of the Dharma.
I beg you to enact your kindness
To accommodate this.

I am the one who admonishes you with advice, but the Sutra on Personal Freedom proclaims:

Those who have learned much
Live in the forests,
Living in happiness
When their youth has passed.

Just as we find it here, I seek to search for the meanings of the Dharmas I have studied in a secluded place, so please grant me your permission to do this. This is my request.

Regarding this, while you have already reached the other side in the fields of knowledge that are to be known and have already gained much learning, at the time I write this commentary I am almost thirty years old. My youth has not yet passed, and I am still fresh, so you may think that the time has not yet come for me to live in seclusion. I am not old in age, but I am like an old man due to three Dharmas, so it is fitting that I live in solitude.

You may ask what these three Dharmas are.

The strength of my body is declining. I have become indolent, thinking that while the glory of the Dharma's teachings have not failed and there is a Dharma King such as yourself, which makes it an opportune time for those who wear saffron. The root of the teachings is the Sangha that retains the holy Dharma, and you possess an inconceivable power and ability to help them. But if a great Dharma King who holds the teachings of our teacher dear does not concern himself with them, how could a monk like me, who has little power, be able to help them? I think of these things, but they make me totally depressed, so I wish to live in solitude. These are my considerations.

I have said these things intentionally, so that those who are to be trained will begin to persevere in the holy Dharma, so that they will be multiplied through its many hundreds of merits, so that those Bodhisattvas who have studied many things will not be indolent and depressed about helping others, and so that they will enter it with joy, like geese who enter into a lake of lotus flowers. This is what master Śantideva said:

> Through our merit,
> Our bodies are happy.
> Through being wise,
> Our minds are happy.
> We remain in samsara to help others.
> So why would anyone who has compassion be grieved?

> May the minds of those who are most intelligent,
> On the banks of the reservoir
> Of the unlimited diffusion of the Sage's orations,
> Totally churn with this heart-essence of well-made advice,
> A body of liberation,
> So that the things I have experienced
> May be properly experienced by others.

> I have summarized them properly,
> So that they may be expanded upon,
> And so that all living beings may practice them.

> These are scriptural traditions that are stainless.
> They are the knowledge of the omniscient ones.
> They are totally beyond the intellects of the childish.
> They are profound and vast.

> I beg the most wise to be patient with someone like me,
> Whose intellect is inferior,
> Who is incapable of scrutinizing these things,
> And who is deluded.

> What if my survey is not proper,
> Due to my not understanding
> The full extent of these excellent orations?
> Will all these living beings,

Who seek your proclamations in full,
Be left out?

This is the reason I have exerted myself strenuously,
In keeping with these orations as they have been given to me,
And have organized this into a letter,
So that the good statements of the holy ones will not be forgotten.

This book is a worthy summary
Of the heart-essence of all the orations.
In an effort to make these proclamations clear
I have made this ornament to illuminate
These excellent orations.

So it is that this holy companion in virtue, whom we have all accepted, a king of the Dharma who guards well the kingdom of the mighty Sage's Dharma and maintains a perfect store of excellent knowledge that cannot be stolen, who has been empowered, without impediments or attachments, into all the vastly diffuse orations of the Sugata with no exceptions, who has the great compassion to love all living things as if they were his only child, has persevered in organizing a very large populace towards a condition that is truly lofty and definitely good.

He wrote this due to the repeated requests of the great lord of the earth, one who protects the kingdom in keeping with the Dharma, Kublai. It is a summary of the significance of all the excellent orations of the Sugata. It teaches the way that they are to be taken into our experience. It is An Ornament to Illuminate the Orations, an explanation of the Excellent Work of Advice for the King.

Having touched the filthless feet of this holy guru, and savored the ambrosia of his explanations, a Keeper of the Baskets by the name of Sherab Shonu, in keeping with the instructions of this holy guru, compiled it in full at the library at the residence of Tsumdo[39] in the year of the female wood pig (1275-76 A.D.) during the mid-month of autumn on the twenty eighth day. He then met repeatedly with that same one[40] to correct it.

---

[39] Tsum mdo
[40] Chogyal Phagpa

Chogyal Phagpa

AN OUTLINE OF MY ADVICE TO THE KING

rGyal po la gdams pa'i bsdus don

I bow to the Lord of the Most Wise, the ever-youthful Mañjuśrī.

The Brilliant Work of Advice to the King has two parts: The actual advice regarding the holy Dharma and an occasion to address casual concerns.

There are three parts to the first of these: The heading that begins the composition, the actual content of the composition, and the final ending.

The first of these has two parts: A statement to truly honor our teacher and the promise to give an explanation that eliminates two kinds of erroneous presentation.

The actual content has two parts: Speaking out on the Dharma and advice for practicing it.

The first of these has three parts: A teaching on the requirement that we take the meanings of the Orations we rely on into our experience, the way to take them into our experience, and the result of taking them into our experience.

The second one has two parts: An expansive explanation, which is a summary of all the Dharmas of virtue, and then a summary that presents the necessity of perfecting each individual Dharma of virtue.

The first of these has five parts: Purity in the rule of the way, which is the basis of the path; the contemplation on our motivation, which is a preparation for the path; the yoga of placing ourselves into equanimity, which is that actual foundation of the path; the follow-up activities, which augment the virtues of the path; and the stamping of all the paths and the Dharmas with seals.

The first of these has three parts: The vows for personal freedom, the generation of a Bodhisattva's attitude, and a presentation on the benefits of protecting it.

The generation of the Bodhicitta has three parts: Compassion, determination, and our ability to succeed. These three show the causes for its development, the way that we take it up in purity, and the methods for using it to reach the end.

The second one, the preparation for the path, has two parts: An extensive explanation and a summary.

The first of these has three parts: Faith, which is both something that is associated with the object that causes its development and is a way to meditate; compassion, which is both a teaching by analogy and an application of our visualizations to our purpose; and the generation of a longing, which refers to both the object that we long for and the way that we are to long for it.

Third, the actual practice of settling into equanimity, has two parts: An extensive explanation and a summary.

The first of these has three parts: Meditation that uses visualizations, the teaching that the mind is the root of samsara and nirvana, and the way that this is to be taught: The way to investigate it, and the settling into equanimity regarding the significance of this investigation. These three are used for meditation without visualizations.

These three are used for our meditation on interactivity: The interactive nature of things, the teachings on the inner character of every Dharma, and the way that we put ourselves into equanimity.

Regarding the use of visualizations, there are two parts: The primacy of the intended object and the inclusion of the place and retinue.

We use three methods of offering honor to meditate on the Buddha. We meditate on our guru using these four: The true nature of our intended object, the time during which we meditate, the abode on which we meditate, and the way in which we meditate.

The follow-up after these four has two parts: An extensive explanation and a summary.

The first of these has three parts: A general presentation on reasons, advice on what must be recollected upon doing a virtue, and applications to follow our settling into equanimity as the occasion allows. There is the requirement that we do a follow-up recollection on the benefits in this, so we use the four higher perceptions as they come to us.

Then there is the dedication of our virtues. We use these two: What a dedication is and what its benefits are, to make a prayer.

The fifth one, the stamping of all things with a seal, has two parts: An extensive explanation and a summary.

The first of these has three parts: That relative reality is like an illusion, that ultimate reality has no true nature, and that their nature is to be interactive. The knowledge of this is an amazing abode, as are the way in which we understand it and the advice on what to do to perfect it. The essential interaction between these constitutes a fourth.

The first of these has two parts: Four distinctions, four specific Dharmas, three analyses to present an analysis of compounded dharmas, that our ideas about language are in fact compounded, and three teachings to show that the idea that substances exist is a delusion, which is a presentation on the uncompounded: That we must not ignore karma and its fruition, and a presentation on the areas that are deviant.

Secondly, that the ultimate reality has no true nature, there are three parts: Rejecting the designation of it as being a delusion, and the way to put ourselves into equanimity regarding its uncomplicated nature.

The first of these has two parts: Using the two refutations of unity and plurality to refute the existence of external things with these four: Refutation of existence, refutation of non-existence, refutation of both, and refutation of neither.

I refute the Nyāya. There are two parts to this: A statement on the ancient positions, an analysis of unity and difference, that when an object is not established a subject will not be established, and a refutation of the belief that there is something other than them.

The third, the result of taking this into our experience, has two parts: Bringing it together and the real objective, which has two parts: The truly high and the truly good.

There are two parts to this: Temporary fruitions and ultimate fruitions.

The first of these has two parts: The path of accumulation and path of application are used for the temporary conditions of the world. The path of seeing and path of meditation are for temporary conditions on the path of the noble ones.

There are two parts to the ultimate fruition: The teaching on using the path that reaches the end to accomplish our fruition, and on the embodiment of true nature, the embodiment of perfect pleasure, and manifest embodiment.

We use the four teachings that these are an unceasing continuum to bring a real fruition to our practice.

The second topic, the things that come up causally, has three parts: Bringing things together, the request that you listen, and the real topic.

This has three parts: That your life be lengthened, that the glory of your hereditary descendants be stable, and a request that you use methods to realize total liberation. These three are directed to you personally.

Then there are requests for the sake of the teachings in general.

Then there are specific requests for myself individually.

Through the virtue there is in composing
A summary of my brilliant work
On the teachings of the supreme vehicle,
Which let us accomplish a great purpose,
May all living beings become kings of the Dharma.

This elucidation of the meaning in summary form of the Brilliant Work of Advice for the King was composed by the author of that work in the year of the female wood pig (1275/76 A.D.), on the twenty-fourth day of the month of the hawk during the daytime at a place in the land of Tre called "The Residence of Ganden."

The secretary was Atsara.

Advice to Kublai Khan

Chogyal Phagpa

ABOUT THE TRANSLATOR

Christopher Wilkinson began his career in Buddhist literature at the age of fifteen, taking refuge vows from his guru Dezhung Rinpoche. In that same year he began formal study of Tibetan language at the University of Washington under Geshe Ngawang Nornang and Turrell Wylie. He became a Buddhist monk, for three years, at the age of eighteen, living in the home of Dezhung Rinpoche while he continued his studies at the University of Washington. He graduated in 1980 with a B.A. degree in Asian Languages and Literature and another B.A. degree in Comparative Religion (College Honors, Magna Cum Laude, Phi Beta Kappa). After a two year tour of Buddhist pilgrimage sites throughout Asia he worked for five years in refugee resettlement in Seattle, Washington, then proceeded to the University of Calgary for an M.A. in Buddhist Studies where he wrote a groundbreaking thesis on the Yangti transmission of the Great Perfection tradition titled "Clear Meaning: Studies on a Thirteenth Century rDzog chen Tantra." He proceeded to work on a critical edition of the Sanskrit text of the 20,000 line Perfection of Wisdom in Berkeley, California, followed by an intensive study of Burmese language in Hawaii. In 1990 he began three years' service as a visiting professor in English Literature in Sulawesi, Indonesia, exploring the remnants of the ancient Sri Vijaya Empire there. He worked as a research fellow for the Shelly and Donald Rubin Foundation for several years, playing a part in the early development of the famous Rubin Museum of Art. In the years that followed he became a Research Fellow at the Centre de Recherches sur les Civilisations de l'Asie Orientale, Collège de France, and taught at the University of Calgary as an Adjunct Professor for five years. He is currently completing his doctoral dissertation, a study of the Yoginitantra first translated into Tibetan during the Eighth century of our era, at the University of Leiden's Institute for Area Studies. Wishing to bring the literature which has inspired him through his many years of Buddhist study and practice into fruition he has spent the years from 2009 to the present translating the works of the Sakya Founders, a portion of which forms the contents of the present volume.

Printed in Great Britain
by Amazon.co.uk, Ltd.,
Marston Gate.